Praise for Radical V~

"Has specialization hurt customer focus?
divisions of labor? Do you have team mem
Boundy skillfully tackles this ubiquitous c
business principles. *Radical Value* is a gu
aligning their workforce with the goals ....
~ *Michael Houlihan, Founder of Barefoot Wine, New York Times Bestselling Author,
and Workplace Culture Expert*

"As every business goes through massive changes, salespeople need to engage buyers
in a new type of value-centric conversation harnessing personal psychology and value
economics to drive the decision-making process. The book's strength comes from the
author's willingness to make a strong case for demolishing silos and creating a culture
where commitment to radical value leads to excellence and market dominance. This
book is a must-read for any CEO, CSO, VP sales, and sales enablement leader."
~ *Gerhard Gschwandtner, Founder and CEO of Selling Power Magazine, Sales 3.0
Conferences, MindsetScience, and Founding member of the Sales Enablement Society*

"There are literally dozens if not hundreds of books on value, value selling, and the
like. Don't be fooled into thinking that this is just "one of many" and, therefore, worth
passing by. Mark works from high-level concepts down to implementation level details
through the single most important aspects of a focus on value: how it is defined,
measured, and experienced by the customer - and in many cases experienced within
the customer. This makes the book practical, actionable, and ok...*valuable*! Well
done, Mark, for bringing the industry what we need most right now."
~ *Rich Blakeman. Director of Membership, Vistage Worldwide, Inc. Former Sales Vice
President, Miller Heiman*

"Customer service is the epicenter for any business; however, it's more than just how
to provide the best service. It's about providing value for your customers. These two
concepts should go hand in hand, and Mark's book reinforces that principle. It's a win-
win for both customers and companies. What are you waiting for? Read this book!"
~ *Jeffrey Hayzlett -- Primetime TV & Podcast Host, Speaker, Author, and Part-Time
Cowboy*

"If you want to transform your organization, use the "Radical Value" approach with
your team. Creating cultural outcomes that employees connect to will inspire your
people to get into the heart & mind of your customer. Organizations that understand
their customers will get it right, every time."
~ *Jacqueline Jasionowski, Founder, and CEO of Shift Awake Group. Former Customer
Experience Sales Manager, BMW Group*

"I can heavily recommend Mark´s book as he is a passionate and expert in value
selling and pricing. He brings value selling and cross functional interactions within the
company and the customers together with a versatile approach/process that will lead to
higher conversion rate translating in higher buying rates and higher profitability."
~ *Dr. Steve Laborda, Expert, Coach, and Speaker in Value Selling. Former Director of
Corporate Programs, Kemira*

Radical Value provides a playbook for aligning and equipping organizations to build meaningful customer relationships that achieve improved, sustainable financial results. Getting everyone who touches the customer to truly understand customers buy *outcomes* and not the products or services we think we are selling them sounds simple, but in practice is a big departure from where most of us have our enterprises positioned today. These outcomes are personal and unique to our customer's specific situation. A cookie-cutter approach to pricing means we are missing the point of truly helping our customers achieve their desired outcomes, and we miss establishing proper value for our offering. Boundy generously provides us the tools and concepts for success and helps us understand it takes organizational commitment to truly maximize our results. If we use the book as a road map for growth, we will see the journey involves changing our thinking about how value is perceived by our customer, teaching our sales & marketing teams to be experts at gathering data, understanding the personal and business drivers motivating our customer's decisions and developing our options well before even discussing price. In short, it's an exceptional resource for understanding where to lead our teams and how to equip them to build deep, meaningful customer relationships that will positively impact our customer's results and our own.
~ *Steve Sundberg, President & CEO, MedTorque*

"One of the hidden "arts" of selling strategically and impactfully is the exploration, understanding, and delivery of VALUE. Boundy delivers all the perspective you need on how to decipher and deliver value to your clients and position yourself as their trusted resource. Mark himself is THE thought leader on value in all aspects of sales and positioning, and if you aren't following him, you absolutely need to. If you are serious about energizing your sales "game," I highly recommend you reading and absorbing the invaluable content in "Radical Value."
~ *Joe Beck, Founder, The Sales Activist*

"To thrive in business, we need to become constant disruptors and reject the status quo in order to continue to deliver on the mission, vision, and values driving our success and impact. Providing value that is customer-centric is critical to achieving the necessary balance between people and profits. Mark Boundy's book sheds new light in revealing leadership values, conscious capitalism, and performance and shareholder value as complementary concepts, not competing ones."
~ *Tricia Benn, General Manager, The Hero Club, Executive Vice-President, C-Suite Network, disruptor, and agent of change*

"As every business goes through massive changes, salespeople need to engage buyers in a new type of value-centric conversation harnessing personal psychology and value economics to drive the decision making process. The book strength comes from the author's willingness to make a strong case for demolishing silos and creating a culture where commitment to radical value leads to excellence and market dominance. This book is a must read for any CEO, CSO, VP sales and sales enablement leader."
~*Gerhard Gschwandtner, Founder and CEO of Selling Power Magazine, Sales 3.0 Conferences, MindsetScience, and Founding member of the Sales Enablement Society*

"If you are a serious salesperson or marketer, you'll enrich your career by reading Mark's professional sales and marketing book! You'll learn so much to help you close more sales, and marketers will discover how to apply Mark's value-based, customer-centric approach to messaging that Sales needs. Mark has written a book you will refer to for years to come."
~ *Dr. Gary Witt. Marketing Psychology Group, and Professor of Marketing*

Radical Value

Elevate Your Company
— And Career —
by Unleashing the Power Inside
Customer Centricity

Mark Boundy

For information address Goodrich Publishing, 2550 W Union Hills Dr, Ste 350, Phoenix, AZ 85027

This book may be purchased for educational, business, or sales promotional use. For information, please email mark@boundyconsulting.com

Published by Goodrich Publishing
Phoenix, Arizona
GoodrichPublishing.com

ISBN-13: 978-1-7339963-0-3

Library of Congress Control Number: 2020933588

Table of Contents

Chapter 4: Mission Critical: Radically Value-Focused Customer Conversations

Part 3: To Know Thy Customer's Business, Ye Must Know Business

Chapter 5: Efficiently Becoming An Expert In Your Customer's Business.75

Chapter 6: Financial Acumen For The "No-Mathlete" 95

Preface

When I started on this project, I stopped.

I stopped until I had enough to say. So many business books are many pages longer than the actual content delivers...I didn't want to write one of those 250-page tomes with 35 pages worth of information.

So, I held off.

I didn't just want to share the sales methodology I developed. It guides selling to a full understanding of customer value (a fuller understanding than most simple "value selling"), something I've done since very early in my career.

For much of the past decade, I took a deep dive into the craft of selling. I've always viewed selling as a combination of science and art...and as a part of a bigger whole, not a siloed corporate function.

However, my success as a seller stems from my broad-spectrum business experience. As I thought back on the full arc of my business career, I began the process of articulating a holistic view. I approach a major sale with a consultant's eye: toward how my offer solved major business issues.

One formative experience was as a product manager in a culture that relentlessly pursued customer value. I had P&L responsibility for a wire and cable product (pretty commodity-sounding, right?), and I learned value-based pricing tied to value-based product development.

I also held a few positions where an essential skillset was "getting to full speed on a new business and industry quickly." *I learned how to learn* customer businesses quickly so that I could uncover the most value for my offer at the time (including selling money...the ultimate commodity). Teaching the business acumen I'd learned over decades was a natural extension; "Value selling and pricing" joined "Business Acumen for anyone who contacts a customer."

The value culture concept took a major turn as I began to see more clients struggling to sell to executives. I had personally taken this ability for granted, but extremely successful sales performance experts connected "Business Acumen" with high-level sales. This combination also helps sellers know when and how to sell at an executive level...and when to keep their credibility intact by not approaching an executive at the wrong time.

Then a loop closed. In discussion with a couple of CEOs, it became apparent: Companies need to de-silo their search for customer value. *Value focus* changes the buzzword "customer focus" into something that can be operationalized. This isn't only about easy-to-execute tools and processes for sales organizations, (although that's a part of it). It's about radically changing the way *everyone in a company*, whether they touch a customer or not, focuses on value. I wanted to help readers implement *radical value focus* by selling outside their narrow silo.

Doing that closed even more loops. When more customer-facing roles capture insights into customer value and bring them "back to the hive," it enriches functions like product development, operations, logistics, and more. Everyone has a line of sight between their role and customer value.

Now that's worth a book.

That's when I started writing.

I hope you find it a valuable read and invite any conversations it stirs. Reach me at mark@boundyconsulting.com.

Acknowledgments

A book like this takes a large community, and I wanted to thank a few of those who contributed.

To parents who taught me to ask, to ask why, and question what the answer meant.

A whole troop of people at WL Gore & Associates who lived and breathed customer-perceived value…and to an entire troop of people at later companies who used different guiding principles. The contrasts I've had the opportunity to witness have been eye-opening and instructive. I couldn't ask for a more inspiring spectrum of experiences. I learned from them all and am grateful for even the cautionary tales. As the saying goes, "every life has a purpose, even if it's to be a bad example."

Bob Miller, who was a friend and mentor, who gave me the courage to work outside of current boxes and silos.

Steve Sundberg, you may not know it, but you gave me a few small nudges, each at just the right time, that kept me going.

All those great sellers in my past, who gave good examples to follow. Several not-to-be-emulated sellers who showed me (among other things) how easy it can be to game a company's discounting system and earn significant income personally while bleeding their employers white.

Managers who were great mentors and coaches; the ones who lifted me up after my biggest screw-ups…all the way to managers who "taught" me what to do using the process of elimination (only telling me what never to do again).

Alvin LeBourgeois: you were a great example and convinced me that what I have to offer was worth people's time and money.

A small cadre of colleagues I became close to during my years in the Miller Heiman orbit. You know who you are. Thank you.

Jeff Hayzlett, who helped me see when enough was enough, and when to be done.

Tricia Benn: a powerful yet calm force for good in the world. Balance personified.

Gary Witt, who checked my sentences as well as my propensity to unconsciously disrespect marketers, who are becoming ever-more crucial in the B2B customer journey

To Kathy. You are a great mother to my biggest achievement, our boys, and supported me through a lot of learning experiences.

To Tonia. You're a rockstar in your own very different field. You inspire me and showed the faith in me to take this book through its final push.

How to Use the Book

I wrote this with several audiences in mind. While you're welcome to read it as you wish, I wanted to provide some guidance to offer maximum persona-based value (something you'll learn more about as you read).

Based on your role in your company, here are some suggested chapter selections. Boldface denotes higher value:

- Business leader track: You might want to start with the last chapter, 12. It summarizes key findings, and reads like an extended executive summary, then, 1-4 (skim 4 if you are strong in sales methodology), 5, 7-12

- Sales leader track and Sales Operations and Enablement: skim 10, then 1,2-10 (yes, then read 10 more closely, especially Sales Ops/Enablement),11,12

- Seller – *This means anyone who is in regular contact with customers* (technical sales/sales engineering, sales support, inside sales, customer service, tech support, etc.) track: Chapter 2,4-10. At least a skim of the others

- Marketing Track: Chapter 1,2,3-6, 7, 8, (9 if you are involved in pricing), 10, 11, 12

- Product or Service leader track: Chapter 1,2,3-6, 7-12

At the end of each chapter, I will direct a few key takeaways directed at each role.

I am committed to continuous value improvement of this work, like everything I do. Please be generous with your suggested improvements, insults, criticism, kudos, etc. Reach me at mark@boundyconsulting.com.

PART

ONE

A Radically Focused Culture

What is your customer trying to accomplish? Can you answer that question instantly and confidently? Can everyone in your company? What would it mean if everyone in your entire organization *could* answer that question without hesitation?

This book is partly about an answer to these questions. More importantly, it is about how to make sure everyone in your organization knows the answer for themselves and within their roles. Perhaps most importantly, it is about everyone *living up to the answer* to that question in a way that will make your organization more successful, valuable, and long-lasting. Guiding your entire company out of silo-based thinking and focusing them on customer value is radical in my corporate cultures, but it pays dividends.

For perspective, let me tell you about three kinds of companies I often see in my consulting practice.

First, I see and mentor young companies who are intent on changing the world in some way. I call these companies *"living the founders' vision."* The successful ones internalize the world-changing value they bring to their customers. Since employees often have broader job responsibilities – often jumping into very different roles – they experience delivering on that world-changing vision from varying perspectives. It sounds exciting, even just reading about it, right?

As such companies grow, they "professionalize" their operations and management. At some point, they morph into the second kind of company: generic *"for-profit"* enterprises. This is not all bad. For-profit companies can be profitable, sometimes wildly so. These companies are usually effective but become increasingly uninspiring; and, most dangerously, uninspiring to their customers.

For-profit companies maintain/grow the differentiation the founder created for as long as they can. They add systems and structure to the business to run it more efficiently. Departmentalization is mostly effective, with little conflict. "Professionalization" is an inwardly directed initiative, though. These companies can slowly lose sight of what that differentiation is, especially how to maintain/extend it. They often achieve growth by acquisition, combing through Clayton M. Christiansen[1] books or paying substantial consulting fees to figure out how to sustain organic growth.

All too often, companies fossilize into the third type, what I call the "*for-process*" organization. In these cultures, workers think within the boundaries of their job descriptions, which are entombed in silos/departments.

> *It is deceptively easy for executives not to see operating level behaviors as dysfunctional; it can readily be mistaken for compliance.*

Departments become compartments, and silos divide further, then subdivide until they are soda straws. Middle management finds "process" easier to manage than results and reinforces inwardly focused effort. Workers ask managers to help them navigate compartmentalized, siloed department workflows as much as they ask for help with their jobs. In an unfortunate irony, line-of-sight to actual customers is so lost that these cultures invent something called "internal customers."

For great employees, a heavily siloed for-process environment can be suffocating. In fact, the term "great employee" has an entirely different meaning. Ideal workers are those who conform to the system, not the subversive "revolutionaries" who shake things up.

> *I sometimes wonder if the criticism of "entitled millennials" is done out of numbness to an unrewarding work environment. Could young, motivated workers simply be "not sufficiently broken" yet? Not willing to settle for what more worn-down veterans have become accustomed to? Which is the "normal" to which we should aspire?*

For-process companies thrive only as long as their process flows fit their business environments[2] (only a few exceptional processes are flexible enough

---

[1] Harvard Business School professor Clayton Christiansen authored The Innovator's Dilemma and co-authored The Innovator's Solution with Michael Raynor. Both books discuss the reason that big companies struggle to innovate, taking a strategy-centric view of the problem. An alternate view is that there are process and cultural impediments as well.

[2] In one bit of incredible wisdom, Bill Gore, founder of W.L. Gore & Associates, tried to build resistance to "for process" orientation into his corporate culture. In the early days of the company,

to be used in dynamic environments)[3]. As soon as environmental change outpaces the ability to change processes, for-process companies struggle and are too full of drones to understand why results have changed.

For-process organizations often have a strange relationship with differentiation. Using information from a dedicated *Voice of the Customer* (VOC) silo/department, marketers and salespeople try to standardize customer approaches, using the same "differentiated" approach for every prospect.

> *VOC is a valuable concept that can be misapplied. When VOC is a department rather than a corporate value system, you are headed for trouble.*

There is an entire industry built around the pervasive myth of "the magic pitch": the idea that if we just come up with the right message wording, customers will be universally persuaded, and all will be well. As you might suspect, I reject this siren song.

The disconnect between selling company and customer value isn't a middle management phenomenon; it extends from bottom to top. McKinsey & Company surveyed 772 board members in 2013 and found that only 22% of board members understood how their company creates value[4].

The march away from the founder's vision is a natural progression. The failure isn't one of professionalization, though. *The failure is in a lost line of sight to the company's differentiation. And more to the point, how that differentiation turns into customer value.*

At any point along this evolution, leaders can reform into a fourth kind of company culture. This one combines the systematic business cadence of the "professionalized" for-profit company with the relentless focus on customer value found in a "founders' vision" culture.

These companies still have departments and specialties, but each manager connects each role to customer-perceived value. The same set of roles touch

---

he distributed a position paper stating that *it was stated corporate policy to question policies and process*: employees were *expected* to ask "does the policy fit the situation", and if not, every associate's responsibility was to get the organization to forego process and do what's right in the situation.

[3] I recommend The Silo Effect, The Peril of Expertise and the Promise of Breaking Down Barriers, by Gillian Tett copyright 2015. Simon & Schuster. She talks about the anthropology of my "for-process" companies, but Ms. Tett uses the terms silo, the adjectives siloed and silo-ized, and the verb to silo.

[4] I found this statistic in several places, but if you want an eye-opener, read Where Boards Fall Short, by Dominic Barton and Mark Wiseman in the Jan-Feb 2015 issue of Harvard Business Review.

the customer (inside sales, hunters, farmers, bizdev, appointment-setters, trade show staff, installation, customer success, technical sales, demo specialist, service, tech support, accounts receivable, etc.), but in a radical departure from regular companies, *every role* is trained to conduct a basic conversation around value-in-use and can identify a "value gap" with a customer. In fact, everyone who touches a customer is labeled a "seller," even though most don't make commercial offers.

When a culture requires everyone to be a seller, the organization gathers a more complete picture of the customer's world and a better overall connection with the customer. It is common to find opportunities for simple changes with immense customer value, and product developers can innovate more efficiently. In short, the information stranded in today's silos is used to close feedback loops in a value-focused company.

Simply put, these companies focus relentless, radical attention on *customer-perceived value*. Less simply put: read this book.

Gut check – take this one question multiple-choice quiz:

Which of these describes your company's current direction:

> a) we're living the founders' vision
> b) we're operating as a for-profit enterprise
> c) most of us operate as if we're a "for-process" enterprise
> d) we have matured into a "customer value-focused" enterprise

Now, look at your company's current operational and financial results and ask:

If we aren't satisfied with the results we're achieving, is it because we're going in exactly the direction we chose?

A Way Out of the "For Process" Trap for You and Your Customers

Even though a product/service delivers value to many silos throughout the prospective buying company, salespeople focus on the silo with the budget for their purchase. This means that sellers sell only part of the potential value, and buyers buy only part of full value. This org-structure-driven – yet very real – constraint drives all competing offers into the appearance of same-ness.

Taking a radical, value-focused look at your business means taking a holistic value-focused view of your customer's business. Your customers are siloed and are struggling with these issues as well; holistic is radical for them, too. Help your customers take a more holistic, less siloed view of their own business. That sounds like a valued business consultant.

Leadership literature is filled with advice on "how to lead." Too little attention is paid to "where to lead," an issue often restricted to high-level strategy discussions. The "founder's vision" focuses on value for a customer, a really great "where." Radical value focus means focusing your entire company not just on your customer, but all that they value.

In the first three chapters, I will delve into a detailed discussion of customer perceived value; I have tried to distill academic research from many disciplines into everyday language. Any organization – product or service, company, or non-profit – can benefit, but companies who want their offers to be customer-mission-critical should pay special heed.

In later chapters, we will get into translating principle into actionable practice. When implemented in an organization, the practices described throughout this book will form the building blocks of a **radically value-focused culture**. The tools will combine into a corporate competency in which continually growing and building customer value becomes the primary goal of everyone in the organization.

CHAPTER
ONE

The Purpose of Business: Value Creation

The world of business boils down to a fundamental truth: any company exists to generate higher value than the costs to provide it[5]. Thus, we should understand customer value at least as well as we understand our own business processes and costs.

The purpose of any company is to generate higher value than it cost to deliver.

Value is the energy – the muscle power -- that moves Adam Smith's "invisible hand"; it's the unseen force behind all commerce. Without value received on both sides, no transaction would take place. More profoundly, perceived value drives every customer decision along the way; people won't read an advertisement, lift a finger to click on a web link, or agree to a sales call unless they consider each step worth their time. Before agreeing to engage in any part of their buying process ("the buyer's journey," to use a current buzz-phrase), prospects make an internal value assessment; if they don't see value in continuing, the buying process stalls or ends.

When a business generates value for a customer through their offer -- product, service, or solution -- a sale is made. Generate enough value and the seller can charge more than their costs. They can reward their employees for building that

---

[5] Non-profit organizations do roughly the same thing, except their value produced is not measured as revenue. Donors donate when they perceive that value of benefits provided by the non-profit exceeds what they are able to provide directly.

value, forge strong relationships with valued suppliers, and yes, share profits with investors.

When customers perceive a seller's offer as critical to their success in some way, it is perceived as mission-critical value.

Since value is the basis of all commerce, shouldn't we guide our companies by focusing on that basis: value? Why do we complicate business by using so many surrogates and derivatives? Customer value is easy to understand, measure, and track. Why can't we just learn how to use *value* as a corporate guidepost?

> *Shareholder value is a second or third-order derivative of having provided customer value. The same goes for stakeholder value. Customer satisfaction is a first-order derivative. Customer satisfaction is a trailing surrogate. These surrogates and derivatives have their place, but that place is not among an organization's guiding principles.*

Value is the Basis of Business. Now, Make Value the Focus of *Your* Business

Leaders lead by focusing their organization around goals, objectives, shared purpose, or guiding principles – pick your term. That common purpose should be understandable by everyone, intuitive, and reliably give guidance to people in varied roles and situations. I like the metaphor of a compass: easy to learn and use, points everyone in the same direction, and helps people guide themselves out of confusing situations. "True north" weighs into the thousands of decisions and activities that make up daily life in an organization.

When everyone knows true north, the judgment errors become smaller, course corrections become easier, workers can see beyond their cubicles, and silos become less dysfunctional.

Any guiding principle *for your business*, when followed, guides users to measurable (teachable, trackable, and coachable) behaviors that predict business success.

> *Business success is generally measured by some definition of profit, return on assets/equity/investment or the like. A coming chapter will discuss in more detail. Non-profits have additional measures of success, but most of them tie to value delivery.*

I see a lot of different compasses being used in companies around the world, but none focus as clearly on the fundamental basis of business – value – as they should. Leaders can only employ a limited number of guiding principles; organizations need their common purpose to be simple and unifying. Here's the test: When an outsider asks anyone in your organization what the company is trying to accomplish and how they contribute in their role, can they answer clearly and without hesitation? If your set of guiding principles isn't simple enough to pass that test, it/they aren't guiding anything.

Based upon some of the antics I've observed in business, it's apparent that we often lose sight of how guiding principles shape behaviors. Behaviors we often reward don't align with any truly desirable outcome. Here are a few examples of operational behavior and rewards that I've seen first-hand.

- The "Engineering employee of the month" award given to the software engineer who worked the longest hours. His work product was software code, and his managers couldn't measure quality – or test for bugs -- for weeks or months afterward. As a substitute for measuring "quality code," they measured the number of hours his computer was logged onto the company network, plus when his employee badge had entered the building on weekends. His value to the company was his measured willingness to sacrifice his personal time.

- A performance bonus was awarded to the Sales Development Rep, who completed the most telephone dials. It turned out that he let the phone ring once: just long enough to trip the call counter, but not long enough for anyone on the other end to even pick up. Don't start feeling superior, people: the number of other activity-based metrics I see in sales organizations is alarming.

- The purchasing staffer who left critical criteria off of an RFP because too few suppliers could comply; her justification: "if I include that, we won't get three responses." Success was measured by the number of suppliers submitting a bid, not whether any proposal met her company's needs.

- The in-house counsel who "proved his worth" to the company by being a hard-nosed positional negotiator on every agreement, no matter how low the company risk, the quality of the pre-existing business relationship involved, or the time-urgency of the project. The number of weeks it took to get agreements completed was his measure of "thoroughness."

- A sales leader builds a commission structure on gross sales dollars, not gross profit dollars, because "it's too hard to measure profit dollars in our company." Now, an entire sales force is off training the whole world to expect deep discounts. Then, the CEO backs the sales leader up, beaming about revenue growth during the next earnings call, with some story about "we'll make it up on volume," or "This quarter we sold mostly razors. Wait until you see all the blade sales coming up", or "This was about acquiring new logos; we'll gain it back on renewal/services/subscriptions." While any of those justifications might be valid if true, in many cases, they are an earnings-call fig leaf over "discount addiction."

Reading into these situations, what guiding principle do you think is in place for an organization rewarding such behaviors? Are they evidence of maximizing shareholder or stakeholder value? Being customer-centric? Living the founders' vision? Being a for-profit enterprise? Having a discernable direction of any kind at all? Instead, these are signs of companies who have settled into being for-process: doing what makes their silo-based metric look good[6]?

These are symptoms of a significant guiding principle problem – a corporate-level issue: does leadership define "success" in a way that helps the company grow and thrive? If your organization had the right "true north" for its compass, it certainly could.

If a worker can't use the corporate compass to see what "good" looks like for their particular job, the compass is useless to them. Everyone in the organization should be able to connect their role with true north and identify behaviors that contribute.

What is the Core Principle of Your Business? What are the Alternatives, and Which Is the Right One?

Throughout history, business leaders have sought a unifying core principle for their organizations. Here are some of today's options:

- Values centered: defining, then focusing on what the company "values." Values can be around internal culture, moral principles, vision for the organization's place in society, etc.

- Maximizing shareholder value. Weighing decisions through the lens of increasing the value of a (public company's) stock price.

- Stakeholder analysis; broadening shareholder value to all groups of interest, employees, customers, suppliers, etc.

- Being "customer-centric." Focusing on the customer...something about the customer, anyway.

---

[6] If you know anyone with an engineering background, ask them what bad stuff can happen if you optimize a design at the component level rather than at the system level. Then tell me why it's such a good idea for a company to optimize at the silo level. I'll hang up and listen...

These all have their charms...and their challenges. Which one is "best"? Which fits your business situation? Let's compare/contrast the pros and cons of the major options.

"Values" Driven Culture: Value Makes Values Work Better

Company culture experts promote "values-centered leadership and corporate cultures" (very different from being *customer value* focused, the topic of this book). "Values centered" encompasses many different "values," usually promotion of moral, societal, and humanistic principles. I support a strong internal culture, moral principles, and vision for the organization's place in society.

That said, many "values" strike me as "how to lead" but not "where"; they should take their place alongside, but *not instead of* "where."

Combining most moral/social/human values alongside the "where" compass of *customer value* creates a powerful synergy. I have never come across any *values* that conflict with the pursuit of *customer value*.

Shareholder Value: A Trailing Indicator, Not a Guiding Principle

I'm all for having share values rise, but shareholder value isn't a good day-to-day guiding principle.

The idea that a corporation's goal should be to create shareholder value has dominated management dogma for decades. It has recently started gaining the discredit it deserves. The decline of shareholder value is gaining momentum, with scholarly articles in academic journals, the business press, HBR, and the like. For example, Cornell University professor Lynn Stout has written one of the more notable works on the topic[7], stating (academically) the *"the ideology of shareholder value maximization lacks solid grounding in corporate law, corporate economics, or the empirical evidence."* Her work makes two separate but critical points. First, she exposes the flaws in both the legal and economic reasoning underpinning shareholder value. Her second point is even more significant – it drops academic complexity and gets to the real point:

Managing to shareholder value doesn't work.

Once you think about it, this makes sense. Shareholder value is a result of a result (of a result?), a second, or third-order consequence. **Shareholder value is a highly desired result, but not a tool for management.** Imagine a college

---

[7] The Shareholder Value Myth. How putting shareholders first harms investors, corporations, and the public. Lynn Stout copyright 2012 by Lynn Stout. Berrett-Koehler Publishers.

football quarterback using weekly coaches' poll rankings (rather than down and distance, defensive alignment, game clock, and the like) to decide an audible play call during a game. Too many things out of the team's control go into share price – oops, poll ranking. Rankings and championships are second and third-order results...even great goals...but not in-game guidance. Managing a business day-to-day toward an outcome as subjectively determined as share price is just goofy.

Stakeholder Value: More Balanced, More Ambiguous

The shortcomings of shareholder value drove some business thinkers to expand from a single to multiple stakeholders. Rather than throwing out shareholder value analysis, stakeholder analysis tried to fix shareholder value by augmenting it. This draws attention to the conflicting forces affecting all companies which are ignored in the shareholder-only model.

Stakeholder value tries to balance shareholder interests against those of employees, suppliers, customers, communities, and other groups who have a stake in the organization's success. Looking at the broad sweep of different stakeholders and balancing interests will steer a company away from the excesses of shareholder value, which is good.

Stakeholder value purposely adds groups with sometimes-conflicting interests into the mix and asks managers to balance different needs – or come up with innovative win-win solutions, or if you're a fan of **Conscious Capitalism**, win-win-win solutions.

> *One of the four pillars of* **Conscious Capitalism** *is stakeholder focus, the others, higher purpose (there are higher purposes than merely profit), having a conscious culture and great leadership, are all consistent with what you will be learning in this book. In fact, by developing a value focused culture, you may find actionable ways to live up to the Conscious Capitalist credo.*

The challenge with stakeholder analysis is that it doesn't give any prioritization or tie-breaking scheme when interests collide. The appeal of stakeholder value is that it forces more perspectives; the challenge of those additional perspectives is that they can create ambiguity.

Another challenge arises when stakeholder value is measured using trailing measures. Not many metrics predict (or are leading indicators of) successfully balancing stakeholder interests. Thus, you can only measure progress after it's too late to change.

I'm a fan of Conscious Capitalism and all four of its pillars. As it turns out, *radical value focus* helps operationalize the Conscious Capitalism manifesto.

Beyond Shareholder and Stakeholder Value: Customer Satisfaction and Customer Focus

Several University of Michigan (the Ross School of Business) professors proposed an alternative to Shareholder Value: Customer Satisfaction[8]. They published a study in which they proposed "(1) customers are the primary source of all future positive cash flows, and (2) customer satisfaction is a significant indicator of the strength of the firm's customer relationships (and thus the timing, level, and stability of cash flows). The authors convincingly correlated customer satisfaction with growth in company value, while making a case that customer satisfaction is a more powerful long-term goal. This makes sense intuitively, of course, but let's follow their path another step or two.

Remember, *customer satisfaction is also an outcome: A result.* It's a trailing indicator; you can only measure it after it is largely too late to do anything about it (other than finding a new customer to do better with next quarter). We should study what causes customer satisfaction and try to steer the company toward those behaviors that drive satisfaction, recognizing that satisfaction itself is a trailing indicator.

What drives customer satisfaction? I argue that it's a customer who perceives superior value. If we could measure a customer's receiving value at any given point along their buying journey, we'd really have something (spoiler alert: this is exactly where we're leading). Here's an example: It's easy to determine the value of the salesperson's justification as they request a first meeting (using the measure "prospect agreed to take the meeting"), but customer satisfaction can only be measured much later.

Customer satisfaction is a powerful, highly relevant metric. It's just not a great in-game compass.

Similarly, "Customer Focus" features prominently in current management literature. It's real-time, and you can focus on a customer everywhere along the customer's buying journey. This makes customer focus a considerable improvement over shareholder and stakeholder value. The challenge: many senior leaders lament at *how hard it is to implement this great idea into actionable steps.* Great customer interaction methods (sales training, methodology, and reinforcement) can bring customer focus to sales but don't bridge to the rest of the company. Similarly, customer service training is a partial solution but doesn't form a clear "true north" for the entire company.

---

[8] Eugene W. Anderson, Claes Fornell, & Sanal K. Mazvanchery. Customer Satisfaction and Shareholder Value. Journal of Marketing, October 2004. Pp 172-185

> *The reasoning also applies when customer service training is scaled up into a full-blown "customer experience" (CX) initiative. CX is a great idea, but even state-of-the-art CX practices don't uncover new value or measure it. Best case CX still doesn't go far enough.*

Another pitfall of customer focus is that it doesn't help prioritize between different customer complaints, opportunities, and suggestions. While it seems obvious to break ties using some measure of customer-perceived value, almost every reader of this book has experienced priorities actually based on "loudest customer," "whiniest salesperson," "highest-selling salesperson," or some other metric. Prioritizing customer value is needed.

> *My quarrel is that this relegates customer value to a minor tie-breaking role in certain situations. If value is how you decide the tough decisions, use it for the easy ones too. Then you are down to one good rule rather than many.*

Merely *listening* to a customer does not produce the same quality insights as focusing on what a customer *values*. What customers say is undoubtedly important, but customers can only ask what for *what they know they want* and can only talk about *what they currently understand.*

> *The list of innovations that customers didn't know they wanted is a long one. I've variously heard iPod, iPhone, Uber, Amazon, television, motion pictures, firearms...you get the idea.*

There are methods to confirm customer-perceived value throughout the customer journey, and to communicate that value deeply and widely through an organization (this is a tease for later chapters of this book). I've also seen the powerful outcomes achieved when they do. This has led me to the new "true north" in business:

Optimizing Customer Value Should be your Organizing Principle.

The importance of customer value – customer-perceived desirability of a seller's offer – is well understood: Columbia University Professor Noel Capon described a "Hierarchy of Organizational Objectives" in 2001, placing "Customer Value" as *the foundational objective*, upon which (in order) are securing and retaining customers, current and potential profits, organizational survival and growth, and finally, (yes, it was 2001) shareholder value[9]. What's

---

[9] Noel Capon, Key Account Management and Planning, The Free Press, (Division of Simon and Schuster) copyright 2001. "The Hierarchy of Organizational Objectives" appears in Chapter 1 as a strategic setup to the book's topic.

radical is *how to operationalize* value focus company-wide. Value focus does no good unless it can be incorporated into a company's operating rhythm using simple tools that replicate best practices.

> *We'll give a more complete definition of value in the next chapter, then dive deeply into the psychological and economic underpinnings.*

In spite of the high-powered recommendations from business thinkers, value focus is not the norm in the business world. McKinsey & Company surveyed 772 board members in 2013 and found that only 22% of board members understood how their company creates value[10]. This means that over 3/4 of boards of directors don't know the reason their companies exist.

> *"A company exists to provide more value for customers than it costs to produce." – Mark Boundy*

---

[10] Improving Corporate Governance. McKinsey Global Survey Results. 2013. McKinsey also did this study in 2012, with similar, but not identical results.

Guiding Principle	Advantages	Pitfalls
Shareholder Value	Familiar to the business world. C-Suite friendly (meets one of a CEO's major needs).	Extreme trailing indicator: Third-order result, filtered through a stock market. Drives short-term optimization. Almost useless for private and non-profit organizations.
Stakeholder Value	More comprehensive than Shareholder value. Drives more balanced decisions.	Varied stakeholder interests create conflict; no clear resolution guidance. Hard to avoid some trailing indicators
Customer Focus	Customers are the source of all demand and revenue. They are the central stakeholder in the corporate lifecycle.	Customers voice varied and conflicting requests. No method for prioritizing or resolving conflicts. Can't be applied company-wide.
Customer Satisfaction	Drives shareholder value/ stock price. Works well for non-public and non-profit organizations.	Trailing indicator, although it trails by less than share price
Customer-Perceived Value	Customer priorities clearly map to company priorities. Can be measured in real-time as a leading indicator. Sales prices and profits can be optimized. Informs innovation proactively. Can be fully operationalized company-wide.	Requires a radical change in thinking. Operationalizing value focus is a change management initiative.

Figure 1.2 Comparing various guiding principles for an organization

Why is Customer-Perceived Value So Powerful?

It can be a leading indicator

You can measure it in real-time—throughout the customer buying (and your selling) process. As a result, you can be alerted to problems in time to redirect effort:

- Customer-perceived value can be confirmed at any point along the customer buying journey, and every point along the sales process. I can begin forming a picture of what a customer values from the very first click on my website (if I can capture that information). If a customer accepts my invitation to a meeting to discuss something about their business, I can begin building a picture of value based solely upon their accepting my invite: something in my reason-to-meet triggered value.

- With an early warning system, you can re-align off-track interactions more rapidly.

- Clarifying unacceptably low-value pursuits early means de-resourcing at a more economical time, enabling you to "lose fast."

- When the customer's perceived value is well understood, you can forecast purchasing behavior much more accurately – and improve forecast accuracy.

- Early understanding of customer value enables high-value innovation. It reduces the uncertainty associated with new/refreshed products early.

- Understanding value perceptions of past customers within a new customer segment allows you to sharpen initial messages more rapidly and accurately – evoking most influential satisfactions.

- Understanding the details of the customer-perceived value of your product or service allows you to tailor persuasive messages around logical and emotional satisfactions.

It can be operationalized

- The behaviors to assess the customer's perception of value can be:
  - Taught
  - Evaluated
  - Measured
  - Tracked
  - And continually refined

When the language of customer value becomes spoken throughout your organization, considerable gains in effectiveness are achievable – not just in sales.

Focusing on delivering customer value Is how the best sellers sell, and how the best organizations grow

Every good sales methodology (sales training company-speak for a type of training) emphasizes uncovering needs and connecting your solution to those needs. That's basic needs satisfaction selling or rudimentary value selling.

There are many trademarked terms for the basic idea of consultatively addressing customer pain-points/needs with customer-centric solutions. Wow…that's a lot of buzzwords in one sentence.

Great sellers get a customer to envision outcomes, then consider value of those outcomes. Elite sellers 1) get customers to measure outcome value, 2) make sure that personal outcomes are included in the mix. Jeb Blount, in his book Sales EQ, makes the point that "people buy for their reasons, not yours." This fundamental principle appears less eloquently in many sales books and training courses. Emphasizing the emotional or personal side of the buying decision equates to selling to personal value.

Here's one element of *radical value focus:* When everyone in your entire company is tasked with gaining insight into why your customers buy, you have a powerful key to de-siloing your organization. The difference between "sales wants feature X" and "our customers will achieve outcome Y when we provide feature X" is profound[11]. Seeing "how we help, viewed through the customer's eyes" helps allocate resources most effectively and set good company strategy. If you offer a product or service that should be mission-critical to a customer, you can't afford to do any less.

The second element of radical value focus is leveraging all value touchpoints in the customer organization. Much more on this later.

Focusing on delivering customer value leads to long-term success

As Anderson, Fornell, & Mazvanchery asserted in their customer satisfaction study, the source of all revenue is customers. The source of repeat revenue is satisfied customers. Here's a catch: value received by a customer is important, but value *recognized and internalized* by the customer is critical.

Delivering great value helps optimize pricing. Oh, …and profits too.

Profitability comes from consistently delivering value in excess of your costs – then realizing that delivered value in the form of price. We'll cover the ability to charge a profitable price in great depth in future chapters (especially chapter 9). Remember this, though: what it costs you to provide value should not be your customer's problem. If your value only warrants an unprofitable price, you own that problem – every customer ever will tell you so. By the same token, if your offer is wildly valuable to customers, your cost to deliver it is none of their concern either. Making them happy about the price is a simple matter of helping them justify value to themselves.

---

[11] Tett, Gillian. The Silo Effect. The Peril of Expertise and the Promise of Breaking Down Barriers. Simon and Schuster, 2015.

A quick observation about cost-cutting

Cost control is good corporate practice, but it has limits. Cost control, what one of my first bosses called "frugaling" takes energy and management focus. Cost-cutting your way to profitability is one of the hardest ways to increase net income. Combining cost-control and growth is even harder:

You can't shrink your way to growth.

When you start cost-cutting, it's challenging to maintain customer service and responsiveness levels. It's hard to provide a helpful, cheerful voice to your customers when they call in. It's hard to innovate. It's hard to get face-to-face with customers. You are at significant risk of trading customer satisfaction for cost improvement.

Make no mistake: times sometimes get hard. For example, if you sold capital equipment into the oil & gas industry during the oil price slide of 2016-2017, you know that there is sometimes no alternative but to "right-size" in response to an uncontrollable market dynamic. When you go through this struggle, though, don't mistake right-sizing for a growth plan.

More importantly, don't mistake a cost-cutting project for a guiding principle. Keen awareness of customer value can guide you through prudent cost-cutting (could you say the same of shareholder value focus? CustSat scores?), but cutting costs isn't a way to produce customer value.

Pricing to value grows profits

Let's examine a different path to profitability: Pricing profitably. Any executive realizes that pricing power is the strongest lever to drive profitability. Unfortunately, most executives often wonder if their sales forces are equipped to take advantage of the pricing power they have. In my experience with hundreds of sales forces, these suspicions are well-founded. With pricing power, a little bit goes a long way on your bottom line. The trick is avoiding customer alienation sometimes (but not automatically) associated with higher prices.

In the long term, customers only give you pricing power voluntarily. If a customer doesn't feel your offer is fairly priced, they will find a way to even the score…and they often don't stop at "even": lost referrals, follow-on opportunities, and more are the ways they take their revenge. Your sales force must have the tools to help customers feel good about the prices they are paying. It's not only possible. It's teachable, coachable, and repeatable.

Delivering value to a customer is something. Knowing what value your customer believes you deliver is everything.

Pricing Leaders: You can only price to value if your customer believes it's in their best interest…that is, believes the value warrants it. Customers need a clear picture of value to make a clear decision on the fairness of your price. Sellers need to know when that value is there, when it isn't, and how to grow it – in the customer's mind. When your teams can clearly articulate the components of overall customer-perceived value, everyone in your company can contribute to opportunity pursuits.

"Pricing courage" based on gut feel or bravado is posturing – possibly foolhardy. Pricing after you know the value you provide takes no courage at all…just sound, coachable conversation behaviors.

A thorough examination of your value conducted with your customer leaves them feeling better about the bargain they received. Appreciating the bargain they received translates to preference, resistance to price pressure, and ultimately loyalty. This is at the core of how you deepen customer relationships, both for increased sales, and increased account defensibility.

Business Leaders: If your people don't price to value, how can you afford the costs it takes to keep delivering it? What will give you confidence that your price – "high" or "low" – is sustainable? Because a customer only pays a premium price voluntarily, you need to know how customers value your offer before you can make informed decisions to invest in service, innovation, efficiency, etc. Staying tightly in tune with the value provided to your customers means never having to say, "our customers changed from under us."

> *At least in the long term -- the most important time frame of all, unless you're suffering from "shareholder value-linked quarteritis."*

When your product developers understand how your customer achieves value from your product, they can come up with more targeted, value-producing innovation.

Value can become a common language and a common cause for or your entire company. Let's contrast the five examples at the beginning of this chapter. Consider the difference of value-focused organization vs. the examples at the beginning of this chapter:

- Instead of "hours at your keyboard," the software engineering team recognizes contributors who develop customer-valued ideas. With a direct line-of-sight to customer value, contributing to a key customer outcome can be rewarded.

- Rather than being rewarded for dials, or even appointments set, SDRs are rewarded for unearthing differentiated customer value drivers to be explored in sales appointments.

- Because value focus permeates a company's culture, the person assembling the RFP understands why forcing a value-reduced decision on her own company is harmful and produces a request that accurately reflects the buying organization's needs, and makes stakeholders available to discuss the nuances of value. I'm well aware that some RFPs are fig leaves for already-selected suppliers, gambits to grind an incumbent for price concessions, or collection devices for free consulting, etc. To the extent that the organization is open to creative value addition, procurement organizations should welcome it more frequently than some currently do.

- The in-house counsel who is sensitive to the business value of agreements in his care and is able to become a business resource and a decision partner.

- The sales leader develops a profit-related compensation system using approximate profit (because "actual profit" was too hard to measure," remember?), then gives his sales organization the ability to sell value-based prices. The CEO can crow about profits on his/her investor calls, instead of "just wait"ing.

The Verdict: Customer Value Should be Your Organizational Way of Life. That's Radical

Maximizing customer-perceived value as a guiding corporate principle is a more effective business model. It's easier to differentiate, easier to have pricing power, easier to generate profits, easier to become a trusted partner with customers, and easier to build long-term customer loyalty. I'm pretty sure that most shareholders will be OK with that.

With radical value focus, you can build *a culture of continuous value improvement.* When everyone has a line of sight into customer value, and any process or product improvements are viewed through a lens of "how does this affect customer value?" people ask the right questions more often, your customers see more value in what you provide.

Key Take-Aways

Corporate Leaders: I know it's radical, but focusing everyone in your organization on customer value is a guiding principle that breaks down silos and helps everyone focus on the most important thing in your business: your customers' outcomes. Installing customer value as "true north" requires a well-considered change management plan, but you'll find it's one that appeals intuitively to everyone in your company. The most significant barrier may be you not believing that your people are up to it.

Leaders in Sales, Sales Enablement, and Sales Operations: Value focus helps you prioritize opportunities, improve customer interactions, increase win rates, and forecast accuracy. You will need to implement a consistent coaching and management cadence around value, which could be a few simple tweaks to your existing sales methodology...or a monumental culture shift.

Sellers (by this word, I mean every role that interacts with customers): learning how to have great conversations around customer value will help you become a valued resource and trusted advisor to your customers. This builds the best kind of customer relationships

Marketing Professionals: Every tool in your arsenal is more effective when you communicate in terms of customer outcomes. Frustrating discussions with sales become much more collaborative when customer value is installed as the common goal of all parties. Account-based marketing becomes highly focused and effective. Content becomes more impactful.

Product/Service Professionals: Your product/service roadmap is better informed, and there is higher confidence in what to include/accelerate and exclude/delay. With an accurate value assessment, you can make more precise pricing and costing projections. Your product training materials are no longer feature dumps, but full briefings on the customer's value-in-use, personas affected, and proposed value to each.

CHAPTER
TWO

What is Value?

The word "value" means many things to many people. My goal for this chapter is to make sure we provide a clear definition and describe the psychological underpinnings of value. First and foremost, we need a common understanding of "the V-word."

> _Value is the customer-perceived desirability of an outcome (or group of outcomes) associated with some course of action. (Note: Status quo is a course of action too)_

Let's break that down, starting with outcomes. When a customer buys from us, they are buying something other than the product or service on the order.

> _No, they aren't "buying you." Your credibility is critically important, but slavery is illegal. I understand the reason for that old saying: it's a bromide meant to emphasize the importance of credibility. Credibility affects their belief, or how strongly they anticipate outcomes, but outcomes are what value is about._

A significant influence on my professional life, Bob Miller, founder of Miller Heiman, was known for saying:

> **Customers don't buy products or services. They buy the outcomes they anticipate those products and/or services deliver.**

In reviewing my value pricing material (one of my training offerings) with Bob several years before his death, he was pleased when I took his mantra a step further:

What customers are willing to pay for those outcomes is based upon the perceived, expected value of those outcomes.

So, value is the desirability of those outcomes – in the customer's perception (customer's outcomes, customer's desire for them). If the course of action is "buying from you," then the value is the desirability of the outcomes that buying from you will yield.

The immutable law of value states that:

Value exists only in the mind of your customer.

Throughout this book (and for the rest of your life), value is a mental picture in another person's head. It isn't something you can experience, feel, or measure – unless you're the buyer. When you hear "value," ponder the top half of a customer's head and trying to figure out what's inside. Introducing, changing, and building value all happen between a customer's ears, guided by you, your company, your marketing content, and your sellers.

The study of value overlaps with psychology and economics. It's also the application of soft skills; if the value is only in your customer's mind, the most critical personality traits for a value practitioner are empathy, engaging dialogue, and listening ability.

Basic Decision-Making Processes Around Value vs. Price

I've maintained an interest in consumer choice behavior, and for those interested in dipping their toes into an accessible summary of some of these principles, I recommend the podcast series "Two Guys On Your Head[12]," put on by Dr. Art Markman and Dr. Bob Duke at UT Austin. In one, they sum things up well: "We look for efficient ways to get on with it. That's what brains do[13]" This means:

- People will choose quick ways to narrow many choices down to the finalists: usually two. If you are in "the beauty contest" phase of a significant proposal to a prospect, rest assured that no matter how many contestants are invited to present, mentally, everyone – and sometimes the group – narrows things down to a final two rapidly.

---

[12] http://kut.org/term/two-guys-your-head

[13] Two Guys on Your Head. In their Podcast "Choice", Jan 14, 2016. I also recommend "Discussion of Behavioral Economics-Kahneman and Tversky". I recommend http://freakonomics.com/podcast/men-started-thinking-revolution/ for even more background. Pick up anything by Tversky, Kahneman, or Richard Thaler.

- Individuals and groups then go into a more detailed decision process to choose between those two. In the decision between the final two, small differences, including emotional/personal ones, start to loom large.

- At almost no time during this entire process does anyone devote serious time to similarities; In complex buying decisions, there is often somebody whose job it is to screen for "minimum fit": making sure all serious options "meet the spec" or perform similarly. This is "differentiation" only in the most tortured sense, narrowing to a group of options that meet a "table stakes" standard.

  Table stakes started as a poker term. In business, table stakes are the minimum entry requirement for a market or business arrangement.

- The combined value of any outcomes that the customer finds essential – a value premium – is used to counterweight any price differences.

If the value premium outweighs any price premium, the premium-priced option is selected. If the value doesn't exceed the price premium, price wins (technically, price doesn't actually win, insufficient value loses. Think about that difference the next time a salesperson says they lost on price).

Remember the principle that humans only work as hard at their buying process as they need to. We'll refer back to it a few times.

As soon as a decision is made, people are ready to move on. Almost nowhere is this behavior more evident than in purchasing decisions.

How Value Grows in the Mind

Let's introduce a simple model of how value grows in the mind of the customer through their buying journey. There are a few more wrinkles when the buying decision is the group consensus buying decision, but the basic process is the same.

Fig 2.1 How value grows. Note: the right-hand box, value development, will be expanded later on.

The Basis of Value: Differentiation

Customers understand your offer – and judge its value – value by focusing on differences. There is usually a lot of sales and marketing work invested in launching a prospect into this process.

> *You would be doing yourself a disservice to ignore the work it takes to get a prospect from "status quo is no longer acceptable," then "what do I understand about my problem," and then into "now how am I going to solve this problem" mode. Value focus is also used to get prospects through these stages, but to understand the neuroscience of value building, I'm beginning in the middle.*

Getting them to articulate a need/gap is the culmination of a significant part of a buying journey and is the focus of many careers. The value of a vendor's offer, though, comes down to perceived differentiation.

This decision behavior is extensively researched and well-validated in consumer research. The human brain is wired to pick out differences and to focus on them.

> Our ancestors, who noticed a pair of eyes peering from a sea of long grass, passed their genetic material more successfully than the hominids who just saw grass. We have perception systems hard-wired to capture contrasts/differences and focus on them when making decisions.

We also develop and use mental shortcuts (researchers call them heuristics). Many of the shortcuts we use are based on either differences or some other source of memorability.

Soapbox moment here: to maximize perceived value, stop telling prospects *everything* about your product! Bypass everything where you and competitors are the same (exception: correct any mistaken perceptions. If a prospect erroneously thinks your offer is missing something important, you need to correct their misperception). Customers "yada yada[14]" anything they believe is irrelevant or unimportant, focusing their mental energy on ways to distinguish and differentiate options. They suppress similarities between purchase options, *even when they value those features.* After examining options to verify that minimum requirements are met, customers expend the real calories on the differences.

Two notes: Some differences, such as brand, are abstract. These differences are real and sometimes powerful. Other differences, like "quality," are

---

[14]Yada, yada: to gloss over, or under-consider. From the TV Sitcom "Seinfeld". https://en.wikipedia.org/wiki/The_Yada_Yada

ambiguous – figure out what "quality" means to a specific buying decision and build value on that.

Differentiation is Not Just One-Dimensional

Value doesn't always have to be derived from a single product attribute. Very often, it comes from being the only competitive option that offers two (possibly common) features simultaneously. I regularly help clients position themselves as "the only option that supplies A and B together."

> Here's an example: A telecommunications equipment manufacturer was designing a telecom product. About 35 very high-speed signal connections were needed between two circuit boards, and the connectors designed to launch and land these signals had already been specified (and there just wasn't enough real estate to accommodate much else); redesign would be so complicated that it would seriously delay the project. There were dozens of low speed/low signal fidelity cables that were available in the market to fit in this connector system. There were also dozens of cable/connector systems able to carry signals of sufficient speed at lower signal density. My company sold the only ribbon cable capable of carrying electrical signals of this speed into this particular connector system.

Since this customer's challenge was a common one, we were able to teach our salespeople to look for this challenge (signal speeds above X combined with signal density above Y).

You can build a substantial business by offering a two-component differentiation. Look how big the market is for a non-drowsy allergy pill, for instance.

I've seen value created for niche or one-off opportunities by being the only option combining three, A+B+C. For example, "the only flooring of its type that has good (although perhaps not the best available) sound deadening, ease of repair/replacement, and is also adhesive-compatible with a particular subfloor system" wasn't something to build an international business upon, but was undoubtedly compelling for one particular project.

That is the Psychology. In Practice...

Remember, differentiation is not about what you tell the customer your differentiation is – it's what the customer thinks the differences are. There is no such thing as differentiation *telling*. When a seller is with the customer, "value messaging" doesn't automatically translate into value (in the customer's mind, remember?). Sellers need to confirm – through a two-way conversation – that differentiation and value formed, and how much.

Conversationally, differentiation is accomplished through questions like:

What do you like about this option versus others you're considering?

How is this different from other approaches you've considered?

Bottom line: be open and proactively seeking any and all forms of differentiation. The more you find, the better.

Value is About Customer Outcomes

If customers look at differences but don't connect differentiators to one or more outcomes, the decision process stops right then and there. Salespeople and marketers need to help customers connect the seller's offer to the buyer's desired outcome. This is rarer than you might think, and why "feature dump" is so ineffective.

Think about it: If a prospect doesn't value what you're selling, no matter how much they *should* love it, it has no value. All value is customer perceived. One of the jobs of the selling organization – the entire organization – is to link their offer to an outcome, then an outcome to value between that customer's ears.

Many salespeople try to get customers to articulate "pain points" and desired outcomes from them. While this isn't bad, such salespeople are looking for the same differentiation every competitor is. In figure 2.1 below, "pain points" are one of four possibilities: customer known and negative. There are other places to look for value gaps and desirable outcomes.

Fig 2.2 Four classes out outcomes. Note: the right-hand box, value development, will be expanded later on.

In contrast, a value-focused organization looks for desired outcomes of many types: known and unknown, positive, and (mitigating) negative. Unanticipated outcomes are ones that few or no competitors expose and sell. Psychologically, negative outcomes are more important to most customers than positive ones, but again, known negative outcomes are the most competitively crowded – differentiation here is often limited.

In combination with the four types of outcomes above, each can be divided into business outcomes and personal outcomes. We'll cover personal outcomes later.

Value is customer-specific. That is, our solutions don't have value. They only derive value from the problems they solve and the outcomes they produce for a customer. Value only appears when your customer anticipates/believes in *and desires* an outcome.

During a customer interaction, connecting to an outcome is reflected through questions like:

> How well do you see this [offer] working in this situation?
>
> I see [outcome] if we do it like this. What do you think?

As Confidence in an Outcome Increases, so Does Value

The customer's willingness to pay depends on their *expectation* that they will achieve an outcome. Perceived value of a particular outcome can increase just by increasing the prospect's confidence in achieving that outcome. Part of the buying process is estimating confidence – credibility-- of the company, the offer, and the salesperson. Customers increasingly discount the value of an outcome when they have reservations about the likelihood of achieving those outcomes. That is, a desperately desired outcome is less valuable when the prospect isn't sure that the result will materialize. The selling company's offer has a higher value as prospects increasingly trust they will achieve an outcome.

I coach my clients to consider their credibility with prospects and strategize how they will grow it with every interaction. Building that credibility not only gets calls returned, requests honored, and claims believed, it gives the sales professional permission to build confidence in the connection between the seller's offer and one or more desirable outcomes.

Marketing communications, customer service (building toward repeat purchase and word-of-mouth), etc. should also build credibility. Thought leadership, collaterals (brochures, white papers, case studies, and the like) trade show strategies, and more...should all have a purposeful credibility-building component.

Grow Desirability of an Outcome

As buyers continue, they visualize outcomes, then engage a mental "want/don't want" process. Buyers decide based upon value they articulate to themselves, which means results/outcomes need to be desired as strongly as possible.

> *Customers will lean on vague emotional feelings if needed, especially in consumer markets. Often, they will build those vague impressions into more solid rationalizations.*

Growing desirability involves increasing the detail of the visualization, and building desirability – again, by adding detail to the visualization.

Seller questions growing desirability of an outcome through questions like:

> What does it mean for [company] to get this [result]?
>
> What would that mean for you personally?
>
> Would it be a big deal if you could [outcome]?
>
> Tell me about any other results you see.

Customers only go into as much mental detail as a decision requires. They will use a rough estimate possible can before expending any mental energy in building a more detailed picture of an outcome. A selling company should influence them to visualize more detail. In any complex/consensus sale, but especially in the case of a mission-critical purchase, sellers have substantial opportunity to build this detail well before any final purchase decision.

The goal: get the customer to go from approximations to detailed pictures – plural, if possible (more results, not just more valuable result)

The End of the Beginning...

Many sales skills and methodologies end at this point in the value building process. If you get a customer to this point in the value building process, you can potentially make a sale. Salespeople are human too, and they'll engage with a customer only as deeply as needed to win a deal – even if it doesn't slow the ultimate sale down.

If a sales force is compensated on revenue, not profit, they have an incentive to stop developing value at this point. If your comp plan makes selling to "just enough to win" value just as rewarding as "selling more value at a higher price," normal human salespeople will choose the former.

Value Development That Wins at the Right Price

With the right training, motivation (and comp plan), sellers can be counted on to develop more value.

Value grows/develops as the customer builds an ever-clearer "value story" for themselves. Remember, people think only as hard as they need to.

> *"Need to" varies by the perceived cost of the item, cost of a bad decision, cost of time to make the comparison. A $1 Mars bar vs. Snickers bar decision doesn't "need" the same mental work as a $1 fastener going into an airliner, for instance.*

If the decision at hand doesn't call for them to analyze your differentiator –or outcomes --in any detail, ultimately in concrete "dollarized" terms, they won't.

The figure below illustrates the value development part of the buying process. It backtracks a little overlapping the "desirable outcome" stage above and then expands the value development process into three new steps. There is an important reason we're covering these four steps as a unit: they start at the first point a customer could be expected to say yes to our proposal. That is, the process in the diagram below represents how value is developed from "just good enough to win...maybe" forward.

Companies practicing *radical value focus* work the value development process described here entirely with their customers.

In the beginning, value is there, but in a relatively vague form. The goal is to get them to progress rightward, toward a value picture that they can clearly articulate to anyone around them, with several outcomes stated in specific monetary terms.

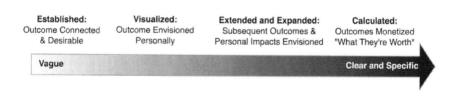

Established:	Visualized:	Extended and Expanded:	Calculated:
Outcome Connected & Desirable	Outcome Envisioned Personally	Subsequent Outcomes & Personal Impacts Envisioned	Outcomes Monetized "What They're Worth"

Vague → **Clear and Specific**

Fig 2.3. Value Development (the right-hand step in Fig 2.1), expanded

Think of a progression, where a potential buyer starts by acknowledging (internally at a minimum, ideally to you) that an outcome is likely and desirable. At that point, value has been established in the customer's mind.

I've studied a bit about the current sales trend of "storytelling." Research finds that a well-crafted story is more compelling than abstractly discussing a list of benefits. Neuropsychologists have even studied the physiology of storytelling:

isolating the regions of the brain engaged vs. regions activated during simple information exchange. Stories activate an imaginative center, causing listeners to project themselves into the story. I believe that conversations that cause the prospect to personalize, projecting themselves experiencing a solution (or closing a gap of some type) engage those same or related thought centers and thought processes. Storytelling is a powerful tool, but a great seller can mix in good conversational alternatives.

An outcome can increase in desirability/value when the prospect walks the next step, visualizing themselves achieving that outcome. This self-visualization creates new neural pathways: the prospect creates a more robust connection to desirability, engages the parts of the brain governing storytelling. This is the neurological reason behind the old saying, "the customer believes what they say themselves more than what you tell them." An outcome becomes more valuable simply through the act of having a prospect describe it – it hardly matters to whom. When they describe it in the presence of one of your sellers, though, they can build a blueprint for any ensuing interactions.

Sellers could stimulate visualization (either with or without the use of storytelling) of an outcome through questions like:

What would this look like for you?

What would this change in your department/role?

As a customer progresses further, they begin to think about all of the ancillary or subsequent impacts of those outcomes: extending and expanding their expected set of outcomes. For example, where a prospect initially describes the time/cost saved by adopting a new software package that automates billing, they may also think of a reduction in costly data entry errors (customer service headaches, slower payments from affected clients, manual intervention in invoices, etc.).[15]

In addition to ancillary *business* outcomes, a person may visualize how an outcome will benefit them *personally*. I once met a sales director who was campaigning for a couple of optional modules to be added to their company's sales force automation program (aka, CRM system); he was very clear with his management that when he was proven right, he expected his judgment and acumen to be taken into account at promotion time. An outcome increases in value as a prospect begins to see these ancillary and personal impacts more clearly. Some sellers call this "thinking after the sale."

---

[15] Neil Rackham, who researched then wrote <u>SPIN Selling</u>, described the selling skill of asking implication and needs payoff questions in his famous SPIN selling book and training courses. These questioning skills work. The *reason* they work is that they stimulate the mental thought process described here.

Sellers could cause buying personas to visualize and extend an outcome through questions like:

> Are there any downstream effects you can see?
>
> If you achieve [outcome], what will happen then?
>
> What would this mean to you personally in your role?

Most major sales training, methodologies, or skills top out at about this point or before. Several talk about personal value, several talk about basic ancillary value, almost none help salespeople look very far out of the selling box for subsequent outcomes. Even when they're billed as value selling, this is about where most stop. I want to take you one further step: looking for out-of-the-box value.

> An example might be a surgical instrument with superior ergonomics. While most sellers can discuss the value of lower fatigue with surgeons, surprisingly few go to HR and risk management groups and talk about repetitive motion injuries and disability claims (which can be common in certain surgical specialties), or to administrators about even tiny increases in the probability of surgical error (medical errors of all types are the third leading cause of death in hospitals – kind of a big deal. Reducing the statistical likelihood, by even a tiny amount, of a staggeringly huge loss event is a great value development opportunity).

Advanced to visualization and extension questions might sound like:

> It sounds like this could also affect [another persona]. Do you know how this would affect them or make an intro so I could ask them myself?
>
> What changes could you predict in other departments?

This step helps turn a run-of-the-mill consensus buying decision by the customer into a mission-critical decision—with you or your seller as the one offering mission-critical value.

Radically value-focused companies and sellers make sure that customers develop the full value of outcomes by:

1. Exploring all ancillary outcomes

2. Going through an exercise of calculating value for each outcome

Calculating value means giving outcomes clear, specific substance in the customer mind: measuring all (or as many as feasible) envisioned outcomes in specific, money-denominated amounts. The key: the prospect performs the dollarization.

Value quantification questions might sound like:

> Similar customers are experience improvement of X. I hate to apply averages to your unique situation. What results might be reasonable in your organization?

If we could change [current results] by x%, what would the impact be for your organization?

What is this problem costing your company now?

What would that mean for you? Your personal life?

Guiding a customer through value calculation is not the same thing as providing an ROI model for your prospect.

- One big difference is that it uses the customer's valuations. Anyone who has ever given an ROI model to a prospect knows the next step, the one I call "battle of the assumptions." Winning that "battle" usually gets the prospect to acknowledge and quantify one outcome.

- Another difference: I have seen very few ROI calculators that delve into ancillary impacts. Little wonder: both sides wore themselves out on the initial model.

- Third, radical value focused companies take the customer all the way through full value development before introducing a calculator. This is because the process of envisioning and self-justifying drastically shortens the "battle of the assumptions." The customer, not the seller, should own the calculations.

- Fourth: monetizing each differentiator follows a common consumer heuristic. Where monetizing conversationally is intuitive, ROI calculators engage a labor-intensive mathematical/logical process.

The Many Buying Off-Ramps in the Value Development Process

Now that we understand the process of value development, let's talk about the likelihood of purchase and at what price. As we stated, a sales opportunity can theoretically be converted to a won deal. That's not the whole story, though. There are three reasons to progress with the customer through the entire value development process:

1. Higher achievable price

2. Higher, measurable customer preference for your offer at a premium price

3. Stronger case for change: better insulation against "status quo," often the most potent competitive option

Both buyers and sellers are human and are prone to "getting on with it" (generally called "satisficing" by decision psychologists/consumer behavior experts). As a result, both parties (seller and buyer) have a reason to get off of the value building process "early."

> *Initially introduced by Nobel laureate Herbert A. Simon, the situation where people seek solutions or accept choices or judgments that are "good enough" for their purposes but could be optimized. There are academic volumes with long sentences and big words, but Wikipedia has an approachable discussion:*
> *https://en.wikipedia.org/wiki/Satisficing*

At each stage, if perceived value is high enough vs. the quoted price premium, a seller might cut a value development conversation and ask for a sale. There is a possible successful sale (a potential loss, too, because value isn't clearly understood). Thus, the customer can potentially take early off-ramps with a buying decision. Sellers have the same "get on with it" motivation and will allow the customer to take that off-ramp for their own reasons.

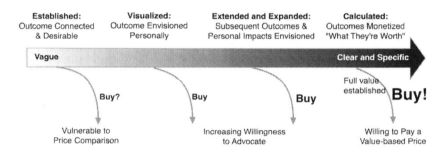

Fig 2.4 Value development process showing purchase off-ramps

Remember, though, that value of a given outcome almost always increases as the prospect internalizes it (describes it to themselves) in greater and greater detail. Thus, value increases at each successive stage. This means that the probability of sales success increases as value development gains clarity. Also, buying preference and achievable price premiums increase as the customer goes through the process. One reason win probability goes up is that as different personas visualize themselves achieving a result, they see good things happening for themselves and become more willing to advocate for that offer to their peers.

Also, as value increases, so does achievable price premium; as value becomes more solidly built in the customer's mind, they are willing to pay a higher price premium to acquire that value. Chapter 9 goes into this in detail, but as the value becomes more evident, more personal, and more measurable, it becomes harder for a competing offer to sway the decision on price.

Simple vs. Complex Buying Process

When the buying decision is simple -- one buying persona, one sales conversation, one single offer/configuration, one price – an old bit of sales wisdom *can* apply. That wisdom is "Don't talk yourself out of a sale. When the customer says yes, shut up and take the order." In other words, let the customer take whichever off-ramp gets the deal done. If there are no peers to advocate to, there is no chance for a competitor to reopen the decision with a last-minute discount, and there is no particular reason to increase the customer's preference (little chance for a referral sale), this wisdom holds.

I've lived my entire career in a different world: the complex buying decision. This world has:

- Multiple personas, each with their own take on value, sometimes with a formal (or at least orderly seeming) decision process that doesn't close until all stakeholders have completed their roles.

- Multiple sales conversations.

- Multiple options/configurations which need to be built consultatively or collaboratively with the customer.

- Pricing flexibility.

- Often, the most compelling "competitive" option is the status quo. The risk associated with change is often a deal-killer.

These offramps are not separated by days of selling work, but by minutes of value-building conversation within a single sales conversation. This is seldom a case where you are running the risk of "selling past the green light." In a complex multi-persona sale, the decision team may not be able/willing/ready to buy yet. Value-building is more likely to build some personas into advocates/coaches/champions who speed the group's buying decision in your favor—and is unlikely to slow things down at all.

The Language of Value in Your Organization

Now that you understand value, let's clarify some language going forward.

Throughout the rest of this book, when you read terms like "customer value" and "customer-perceived value," they will be interchanged with "value." The first two terms are redundant (which made for some interesting conversations with an editor). Since *all* value is customer-perceived, there is no other kind of value. I will use these terms merely for emphasis – and because I overruled the editor.

> *To the "shareholder value" holdouts: Shareholders are customers. The fact that share values are so dramatically affected by imperfect human perceptions is one reason why shareholder value is a poor compass. Stakeholders have value, but they transact time, resources, and goods.*

I want to address another bit of fuzziness that creeps into business conversations: talking about "value chains," "value-added," and the like. Strictly speaking, these should be presumed to be hypothetical value chains, value add, etc.– *unless and until a prospect or customer validates it.*

A "value proposition" is precisely that: hypothesized or proposed value *not yet validated* by a prospect.

"Value messages" and "value statements" are dangerous things: too often, they are value propositions -- unfortunately propped up by a seller's assumption and without the validation step. No matter how well it is articulated in a brochure, no matter how compelling the sales slide deck produced by your marketing group, it's not value until a customer perceives it.

Here is an example of a great value proposition, developed specifically for a valuable target niche:

> A sales performance consulting company has marketing materials targeting newly appointed Vice Presidents of Sales, gently emphasizing the often-brief tenure in this job. "Helping you produce rapid results" is not only a business value driver but relates to a strong personal/emotional one – fear. As strong as this potential value driver is, value doesn't exist until it resonates with a specific newly promoted VP of Sales.

I recommend that companies enforce precision around terminology, using appropriate modifiers:

- "Hypothetical" "potential" 'suspected" are all fine…before a customer has confirmed or validated.

- "Customer-validated" and the like are encouraged to clarify that a value proposition has crossed the "validation line" to become value.

To ensure clarity, these modifiers should be encouraged by executives and sales leaders.

Marketing has a challenging role concerning value. They have a critical role in delivering messages that affect value perceptions. At the same time, they don't always have the opportunity to validate value with customers. It's tempting to claim value delivered without having validated it. On the other hand, world-class marketers help buyers clearly envision outcomes, and painting a picture of the result is a part of the discipline. There's a time to puff and a time for accuracy; decide which is appropriate for you, but please do so purposely and thoughtfully.

> *The term "value messaging," contains the word messaging, whose definition (in every source I consulted) is unidirectional communication flow. "Value messaging" connotes "telling value." The term promotes the dubious practice of not validating or confirming the existence or degree of value in the customer's head. Messaging is fine for marketing, not for sales.*

That said, when you are pursuing precision with prospects, external communications of "value" need a few simple guidelines. Weakening copy by identifying "proposed" and all of the modifiers above isn't practical. Assuming that value has been validated can come off as presumptuous. When in doubt, claim that:

- "Others [just like you] have found this value," success stories.

- "Our solution offers [outcome]"

- "We have found that customer appreciate [outcome]"

- "When customers have been looking for ___ value, we've met that need [insert superlative here]"

- Because of the value of our solutions (specifically___), we have earned X awards and recognitions from Y authority, or Z third party reviews/validation.

Internally, Marketing's function in value discipline can vary. Here are a few themes, therefore we must also use the modifiers above, at least internally.

Regardless of your external language choices, inward-facing communications should incorporate language precision. This helps lead the use of the common language.

Let me briefly speak to consumer markets: In many business-to-consumer environments, face-to-face interaction with individual customers is impractical, impossible, or is the domain of an indirect channel. In consumer-packaged goods, for instance, companies use sophisticated research techniques to gauge customer-perceived value. In this environment, producers assume a "common denominator" value and sell to that value. Obviously, they concede the higher value they achieve in some buyers' minds. The thought process should be the same, but the business model requires some pragmatic modification. Soft drink manufacturers, for instance, segment buyers by the degree of loyalty. Extreme "loyals" will by their preferred brand no matter what, but another segment is prone to switching at some price differential. There is a continuous calculation around attracting price-switchers at the cost of giving extreme loyals a profit-reducing discount (as well as tactical plans to firewall discounts away from loyals).

Chapter Highlights

Some things to remember about customer-perceived value:

- Value is perceived individually. Each person's perception of an outcome defines that outcome's value to them...in fact becomes THE value...to them.

- Perceived value often changes over time, including repeat purchases of the same product or service. Thank goodness. Sellers, innovators, and marketers would need to find other jobs otherwise.

- Value is contingent on differentiation. If you sell the same outcomes that everyone else sells--to the same set of personas—you probably aren't selling value as much as you think you are. You're commoditizing yourself.

- Interesting fact: If a customer believes something untrue about your offer or a competitor's, it's true -- until customer belief in that untruth changes. Unfortunately, misperceptions can be hard to find and hard to change.

- If a customer doesn't yet know some important fact (about you or competitor), that fact can't lead to value until a customer knows and accepts it.

- The value of something grows as the prospective customer first acknowledges, then internalizes, then visualizes an outcome, then considers personal, professional, and business impacts of that outcome, then places a monetary value on those outcomes. The further your organization can help a customer work through this progression, the more value your offer has.

- Remember that the status quo is one of the options that a customer often considers. Sometimes "doing nothing" is your biggest competition, or the comparison/reference option.

- Personal value and business value are two different things, and selling to one in isolation is just as big a mistake as not selling to value at all.

Value is the central concept of this book. Understanding that it's customer-perceived and that it grows as a customer thinks about outcomes and their impacts are foundational to everything else we'll be talking about.

Key Take-Aways

Corporate Leaders: Understanding the importance of customer value is essential, but leading your organization's focus on value discipline starts with language. Applying rigor organization-wide around how value is created in the mind of the customer is a simple, but a never-ending job. In this chapter, I give the core understanding of the customer value-building process and begin laying the groundwork for pricing (and profit margin) impacts of being value-focused.

Sales Leaders: Now that you know where value lives, you can coach your team(s) to help them construct value in the mind of the customer. Understanding value will help you have insightful conversations with salespeople – and customers – about the value of your offer, or lack of it.

Sales Operations and Enablement Professionals: An understanding of how value develops is an important part of the sales training and enablement function. For sales operations, tracking indicators like acknowledgment, visualization, and monetization/justification will give insights into the customer journey that were previously foggy at best. Forecast accuracy and opportunity coaching will improve drastically as you gather value development markers.

Sellers: learning how customers build value in their minds is an excellent guide to constructing great conversations around customer value. This builds trusted advisor customer relationships and commission checks.

Marketing Professionals: Your job is to facilitate the customer journey while creating expectations of outcomes and resulting satisfaction. Creating positive anticipation around a product or service is of critical importance to help Sales. Your job is to facilitate building value in the mind of the customer all along their path, in coordination with all allied selling functions.

Product/Service Professionals: As you build customer use-case/customer application training, inform those materials with an understanding of customer value, and provide the tools for marketing and sales to help customers understand, accept, validate, then quantify the value of outcomes. Product training should be application and value-in-use training, or you are underperforming.

PART
TWO

Why Value Culture Works

In this part, you will learn more about what it looks like to be on a path to continuous value improvement and why "the view is worth the climb."

CHAPTER
THREE

The Radically Value Focused Company

Things feel and work differently throughout the radically value focused organization. With a direct line-of-sight from each worker's job/role to a satisfied customer, a sense of contribution, and clarity of purpose are increased.

A key is to have simple-to-learn, efficient methods to capture and communicate customer value perceptions. These tools can't get in the way of regular work or be seen as an undue burden.

Value Focus Within the Sales Function

Before we take selling activities beyond the sales silo, let's discuss how value focus starts within – and changes – the sales function itself. Sales is obviously a key player since they conduct significant – sometimes a majority of – customer contact. Value acumen in sales is much more than merely world-class selling performance, however. Let's compare commonly pitched sales performance against radical value focus.

> *"Sometimes," decreasing to "seldom." As companies silo the customer interface into more specialized roles, sales becomes a minority shareholder in the customer relationship. Sales will always be highly influential, since they are the ones who present and (yep, sometimes and decreasing) negotiate terms.*

The Basics: What a Good Selling Organization Knows and Does

Before I describe how radical value focus makes the sales function ***great***, I need to explain what good looks like. This section will detail what implementing a robust sales methodology from any top company in the sales performance industry looks like (studies show that these tend to out-perform home-grown solutions, even though they look similar from the outside).

I'm going to also describe the mission-critical sale, the highest level of consensus selling – your world may not have all of these parts, but it's easier for you to ignore some of the elements that don't' pertain.

My consulting practice emphasizes the mission-critical sale, a subset of "complex selling" or "consensus selling," where the offer should become mission-critical to the customer ("should," because many companies "should but don't"). In this area, groups of customer employees in different roles, "personas," engage in a group business-to-business buying decision. As I work with clients to create high-performing sales cultures, we discuss a hierarchy of what goes into a sustainably great organization. I often share this diagram to illustrate the different layers of "sales management acumen" needed. We often work up the hierarchy from bottom to top in a stepwise fashion:

Figure 3.1 The hierarchy of organizational sales acumen.

The Base Layer: Sale Process, Methodology, and Playbooks

This layer is more complex and consumes a lot more energy than the way it's drawn it in the diagram above. In the base layer, many companies develop:

- Sales processes: description of steps in the selling process (a simple process might be prospect, probe needs, demonstrate, propose, close, deliver),

- Sales playbooks (detail behind the selling process including how and when allied functions like marketing and tech support are involved, etc.),

- Selling methodologies (a process to make sure the customer is progressing through their buying process and that sellers' activities are aligned to the customer).

- Documentation

- Salesforce automation: putting everything into a powerful database/time management tool, including contact management, call planning and documentation, opportunity planning, and documentation.

- Account plans

- Territory plans

- Enablement (training, reinforcement, sales content, policies, pricing lists, and guidance)

I could wax poetic about all the parts, but the diagram is meant to communicate that each layer builds on the one below. Training in this layer introduces a lot of desired selling behaviors. Bottom layer training alone doesn't change selling behaviors; behavior adoption is the point of every layer above this one

The Management Layers That Build on the Base Layer, Making it All Work

Once base layer methodologies are introduced to the sales team, it's vital to coach sellers:

- Getting the most out of each sales call.

- Opportunity pursuits (remember sales in this world take multiple calls on multiple people) – coaching sellers through a strategic approach to each sale.

- For their most significant/best accounts, companies should develop strategies to support, strengthen, and grow those relationships.

- A management cadence to review sales funnels (sometimes called pipelines) so that sellers and teams can manage their businesses effectively.

- Once the preceding capabilities are matured, sales forecasting and strategy become much more productive, proactive, and well-informed.

As you can imagine, turning all of this into an operating rhythm in an organization *can* take a considerable investment in a sales culture, and involve a full-blown change management project, sometimes phased over months or years. Sales organizations that have gone through such a transformation will recognize the almost-criminal level of simplification I've committed in the description above.

Adding Value Acumen to the Sales System at Every Level

Now that we've reviewed what good (sometimes very good) sales organizations do to achieve their results, it's time to look at the same system – this time augmented by value focus, at every level.

When companies upgrade their sales system to a customer-value focused one, subtle yet powerful differences yield powerful changes in outcomes. If your company has implemented a good methodology, adding simple value-focused tools is less work than the initial change, but as the diagram below hints, value discipline adds a third dimension to everything you do.

Figure 3.2 Value focus adds depth to the entire hierarchy of organizational sales acumen

The diagram above indicates that value focus adds to all parts of the sales acumen hierarchy. Value discipline adds a third dimension to sales and sales management. It turns vague aspirations of "customer focus" into a sharply defined, clearly measurable management cadence.

Great salespeople uncover differentiation their prospective customers value, then leverage that differentiation to make sales. Sales <u>skills and methodologies</u> are rolled out to describe those selling behaviors, so that entire salesforces reproduce them.

Radically value-focused companies improve on methodologies in three ways:

- First, skills and methodologies are extended. Instead of merely uncovering and leveraging differentiation, sellers are taught and coached through *fully* developing and quantifying a *comprehensive value picture.* Radical value is more comprehensive than most "world-class" organizations settle for.

- Second, *all sellers* (everyone who talks with a customer) are equipped to do the same thing. The breadth of roles that conduct value development conversations with customer personas is a radical departure from today's siloed sales organization.

When entire pursuit teams collaboratively assemble a value picture -- with value fully quantified – the difference in sales and company performance is dramatic.

Some value-focusing methodologies (mine, at least) are modular. That is, they can be added to with just about any base selling methodology. A base methodology only needs to enable sellers to effectively uncover needs & desires (**both** business and personal value) of all relevant personas, then leverage that value.

- Third (for companies that sell business-to-business), all sellers are provided with basic business education to elevate their ability to become trusted business advisors. This enables those radical value development conversations between more of your sellers and more personas at your customer. The more mission-critical your offer, the more important this is.

Value Discipline Throughout the Sales Management Hierarchy

Working up the sales acumen hierarchy, value focus strengthens every layer in the pyramid. Sales coaches can conduct value-focused coaching on

- Call plans: discussing new customer outcomes, developing value,

- Opportunity pursuits (When all sellers collaborate on gathering and building a complete value picture from many facets of the target company, recruiting new supporters, engaging new players, building an outcome-based case for change becomes more powerful.

- Key account strategies (confirming value already delivered, jointly planning new value-producing initiatives, engaging the C-suite on their level).

- Funnel reviews (deeper insights into customer-perceived value informs more focused, more accurate forecasts. When you know more about *why* a customer is motivated to buy, you know more about *whether*).

- Sales strategy, forecasting, and planning (knowing customer value is the foundation for more dynamic/responsive sales strategies).

Sales leadership's ability to coach value throughout the sales acumen hierarchy is a lynchpin in being able to implement value focus in the sales force, and thus in the organization. Value coaching is straightforward – in many ways, it's easier than coaching sales methodology – but it a key to implementing value discipline.

The basics of coaching to full customer value are:

- **Having value-focused conversations.** This is often a simple shift, but a vital augmentation: coaching sellers to conduct quality customer-value-centric interactions.

- **With the right people.** Sales methodology helps salespeople strategize, obtain, plan, and execute great customer conversations. Business and value acumen often open sellers' eyes to new value delivered to additional buying personas likely to value your offer in some way. Thinking outside of the regular ecosystem box is good, but for sellers to identify and target "likely suspects" quickly & time effectively requires general business acumen, it teaches sellers where to look.

- **About outcomes that customers value.** Sellers who understand the principles from chapter 2 – and further detailed in chapter 12-- can use their existing conversational skills to explore, then clarify that value. Coaching salespeople and teams to develop value networks (see chapter 10) is a simple way to not only strategize a single opportunity pursuit, but value networks often apply to many similar customers. Successful/insightful value networks can be "libraried" and curated as a way of replicating best practices.

- **In enough depth for prospects to internalize and develop value in detail.** In chapter 4, we explore why "value selling" isn't good enough. Conversations need to be about all relevant value drivers, but the salesperson needs also to cause the customer to internalize anticipated value and quantify it as much as possible.

- **Being precise about value only being in mind of the customer.** Sales managers must force their salespeople to struggle through the discomfort of looking at the world through a customer's perception.

Another application of value focus in the sales function: opportunity scoring with a value-focused component. From lead generation through successful opportunity pursuit, world-class selling organizations score leads -- and then opportunities -- for fit, or "winnability." Incorporating value into these scoring systems connects an opportunity pursuit to a customer's most strongly desired outcomes. When opportunities with high customer motivation (value) score higher, the organization pursues the highest quality deals.

Radically value-focused companies are not as protective and parochial about customer relationships. Sales representatives no longer insist on being the single point of customer contact. They don't worry about "somebody from the company screwing things up" by saying something they shouldn't. Customer acumen is widespread, and team selling is more coordinated. Risk is controlled by unifying everyone's focus on customer value. Radical value focus is a powerful silo-busting tool.

Perhaps most importantly, sales reward systems must align with value focus. Selling value can be more difficult and time-consuming than simply lowering price. If compensation/commissions/incentives are based upon gross revenue rather than profitability of that revenue, no amount of training and coaching will overcome the wrong message you are sending through a misaligned comp plan. Properly equipped and coached sellers have the most accurate view into achievable price (which is where margins are made or lost). As a result, value focus should be reinforced by rewarding gross margins or similar.

Taking Selling Out of the Sales Silo: Sellers, Not Sales

Over the past few decades, I've seen companies subdivide into functions, then sub-functions, and develop specialties into departments that then subdivide themselves. Sales' role in the customer interface has become diluted as more roles are introduced to "keep sales focused on selling." Ironically, "selling" has been diminished as many trusting relationships have grown in parallel. Everyone who touches a customer is in a position to gather intel for the selling function, but few companies capitalize on this opportunity.

Everyone who touches a customer should be considered a "seller." This requires a radical mindset shift all around.

It also requires some basic, simple (as it turns out) conversational training. Once mindset is shifted, extra-silo sellers are easily taught to ask a few simple questions, bringing responses and insights into a pooled understanding of the customer and their situation.

NOTE: Throughout this book, the word "sellers" means everyone who touches the customer. Sellers and extra-silo sellers are the same things.

Selling Outside the Silo Starts with Business Acumen for All Sellers

I need to take a quick detour to a basic category of knowledge required by any seller engaged with a customer: business acumen. Over many years and many clients, I've found that many sales sellers need to be able to understand an entire network of business processes so that they can predict a more extensive array of business outcomes. This means being familiar with business...business acumen.

As the result of how specialized (OK, siloed) organizations have become, many modern products and services affect a surprisingly wide set of customer departments or functions. Every one of these touchpoints is an opportunity for value...or a point of resistance. Sellers need to understand – even anticipate – the complex web of interested parties their product or service touches.

Here's an illustration of such a web. A batch of medical test strips (faster, used by a nurse at the bedside -- "point of care" in the vernacular -- more expensive than testing drawn blood samples) used by nurses to check patient blood coagulation values proved to be defective, registering inaccurate values. The following groups touched the get-well plan; were involved in the post-recall cleanup action at a typical healthcare system:

- **Supply chain management** coordinated removal by the <u>staff</u> of all recalled test strips from testing centers and found a suitable replacement.

- **Pharmacies, information technology**, and **electronic patient records** teams identified affected patients across all locations.

- The **legal department** created the language for letters and phone calls, as well as talking points/scripts for offices and call centers.

- The **patient records** team generated letters to all patients involved in the recall and automatically added notes to their electronic health records.

- **Staff at anticoagulation clinics** called patients who were at high risk of a complication and arranged for them to be retested.

- **Finance, patient account services**, and **revenue cycle** developed an adjustment process so that patients were not billed for retests or visits.

- **Patient experience group** developed an information base and managed patient questions.

Non-sales department sellers should grasp the business world well enough to anticipate these customer activities, as well as the cost impacts to each group.

If they need to do this when something goes wrong, think of the value they could uncover proactively while going after a sale.

As buyer expectations of sellers have changed, the role of sellers is no longer to provide basic product information – buyers can find that more easily and conveniently through other sources. Sellers need to help customers make better decisions and help apply product/service expertise insightfully to the customer's business... the customer's *entire* business.

Radical Value Focus Throughout the Enterprise

From experience, I can promise you that customer value focus yields powerful outcomes when implemented corporation-wide.

I hope you can envision the value to your company if your extra-silo sales force were to implement a value-focused culture successfully: higher win rates, more defensible wins, higher effective pricing/reduced discounting, higher customer preference for your solution(s).

Value focus introduces a common language on customer value company-wide. Just as the common language of selling methodology yields efficiencies in the sales organization, common value language provides a shorthand to describe differentiation in the only meaningful way: how the customer views it.

Even more important than efficiency, a common language around customer value builds a foundation for a shared *corporate ethos,* which focuses every single employee on the customer and how they view our offers.

Let's look at what company-wide value focus looks like in practice.

Value Acumen in Marketing

Marketing is (or should be) a valued partner for a sales organization. While there are a few other options (sales and sales operations are leading candidates), marketing is a natural fit as curator of customer value insights, no matter what extra-silo seller gathers them, especially since marketing is generally the originator of marketing research – aggregated insights on groups of (similar) customers.

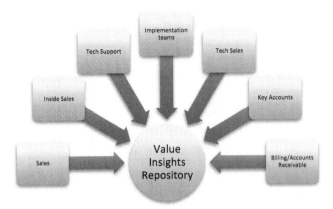

Figure 3.3 Some of the extra-silo seller roles which can contribute to a holistic view of customer value

There is a sales technology, the Customer Data Platform (CDP) that is beginning to mature into this function. Not all CDPs can serve as value insights repositories out of the box, but most are architected to be readily adapted for it.

These insights ultimately inform many processes throughout the company:

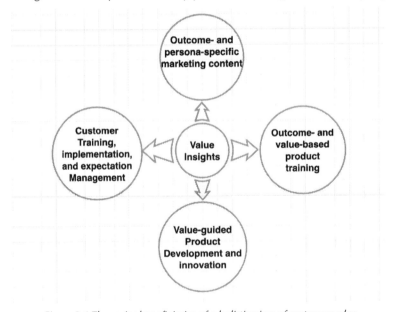

Figure 3.4 The major beneficiaries of a holistic view of customer value

Marketing communication to customers, prospects, and suspects should be informed by careful attention to customer-perceived value. Features and benefits might be starting points, but value realization examples are more compelling and should be the standard. Persona-based communications, account-based marketing, in particular, are fueled by persona-based value studies.

> When I led the first carrier-class, business class VoIP (IP Centrex) platform in the world, we evolved the product and marketing strategy based upon customer value – ultimately promoting the offer into "mission-critical" territory (from a product born as a cost-savings box). Several of the largest phone companies made it clear that their largest Centrex (the highest revenue-per-line service a phone company offered at the time) customers had demanded a service exactly like this, or they were going to defect. We instantly pivoted the marketing/product strategy from "delivering price-reduced Centrex" to "more efficient, flexible, and effective next-generation communication." This then became such an executive priority within these customers that the CEO of Verizon told one of our installing technicians when they ran into each other on an elevator "we're all counting on you to make this work."

Remembering that customers decide only using differences can heavily focus product information/collaterals/content. While product information bulletins must always contain complete product performance data, practice the art of highlighting differentiations and differences which have proved to be pivotal (have led to winning opportunities that you want to replicate).

We'll discuss Marketing's value focus role in more detail in Chapter 13, but briefly, Marketing can:

- Produce outcome-based, value-oriented content.

- Collaborate on customer business profiles (described in Part 3), a quick summary of a company's operations, operational health, and environment.

- Curate libraries and/or conduct workshops to develop value networks (see 0). Some clients have moved this function to their sales operations group.

- Curate libraries of value calculators (or ROI calculators), which are individual customer validations of value, including logical and emotional decision criteria.

- Curate libraries of great value-related sales questions. Note: Some clients have moved this function to their sales operations group.

- Value-based segmentation

Marketing has an opportunity to become the curator of a "value insights library" for the whole company. As anyone in the company (it's usually one of the seller roles) develops an understanding of some customer value driver, somebody in the company needs to maintain a repository. Certainly, a large proportion of this information will be generated as sellers perform their jobs. The selling tools we'll discuss throughout this book simultaneously help sales professionals sell more effectively and capture customer value perceptions.

Once this information is captured (in a CRM system?), it's a valuable database which can be mined for insights to improve:

- Selling strategies
- Marketing support activities
- Product development and enhancement
- And more.

Remember, that uniqueness/differentiation can be a combination of two or more capabilities. I've experienced a large number of these combination plays. Here is an example:

> For a commercial real estate loan, one customer wanted to combine the easy pre-payment terms of a bank loan (but banks only offer short ten-year terms) with the fully amortizing 25-year term of a typical life insurance company loan (which carry punishing prepayment penalties). Even though there were hundreds of banks and dozens of life insurance companies in the competitive space, we were able to give the customer "the only loan with bank-like prepays and a full 25-year term". We won this loan business at a higher interest rate than any of the partial-value solutions. This became a common win theme and became a regularly-promoted offer by marketing.

Value Focus in Product Management & Development Groups:

Product (or service) management groups (sometimes called product groups, product champions, etc.) should be tightly tethered to how customers value the products/services in their care.

For more detail, part 5, but in summary, the role of the Product group is enhanced by focusing on the value of their products' differentiation as they design, plan and manage the firm's products and/or services.

Value focus improves the function of product development. When developers and designers can gain deep customer insights, they are often able to produce superior innovation ("superior" measured in terms of customer-perceived value). When engineers are given a complete view of the customer's mind, they can apply their expertise and creativity in surprising ways[16]. With an alert eye, major innovations in customer value are possible, often at a minimal cost.

---

[16] It's an oldie-but-goodie, however I still strongly recommend the Jan-Feb 1997 *Harvard Business Review* article by W. Chan Kim and Renée Mauborgne, <u>Value Innovation: The Strategic Logic of High Growth</u>. It can be a paradigm-buster.

As we developed the "more efficient and effective communication" value proposition for the first carrier-class VoIP service, IP Centrex, we realized that *without any additional development,* we could create a new-to-the-world (at the time) capability: the virtual call center. By merely selling an existing call center capability side-by-side with our IP Centrex product, call center customers would be able to 1) hire willing workers no matter how far from the home call center they live (this was a major operational constraint in that business). 2) Unify distant call centers under one management system.

The "development cost" of this innovation was minimal: zero product development costs, but cross-training a few technicians, marketing, and product experts, and producing new marketing and sales training materials.

If you or your company is adopting an Agile (or Agile-related) product development methodology [17], or even just the "customer collaboration" building block of the Agile Manifesto, you will find the value conversation tools a great way to turn collaboration into a trainable, trackable, coachable set of operational practices.

Value Focus in Key Account Management

Key account management should not merely be a sales-only function. Defending and growing your best customers requires a coordinated effort, often company-wide. A best practice is a cross-functional strategic planning approach. It is an ongoing, collaborative (with the key account) strategic planning process. Informing your key account planning process with customer value focus gives the process a sharper focus and clarifies many of the activities. With *radical value focus*, the members of your cross-functional team can have value-development conversations with their customer counterparts.

I can't generalize across all key account methodologies, but the so-called "bible of key account management" by Noel Capon places customer value as a foundational corporate objective [18]. Capon's work focuses on evolving key/strategic account management, as depicted in figure 3.5. Where key account management used to be simply an aggregation of the sales opportunities a seller believed they could win with a key account, the focus has shifted to growing the relationship by adding value, which would naturally

---

[17] Agile breaks a big product development project into small, incremental segments, allowing near-constant customer feedback and project adjustment. The Wikipedia page on Agile has a great overview of this huge topic. For the curious, that might be a good place to start. https://en.wikipedia.org/wiki/Agile_software_development.

[18] Key Account Management and Planning, Noel Capon. Copyright 2001. The Free Press (Division of Simon and Schuster). On the third page of the book's introduction, in figure 1.1, Capon identifies Customer Value as a core objective. The entire book incorporates a goal of producing customer value implicitly, but seldom articulates the concept by name.

spawn new sales opportunities. This is the Value Multiplier in action: adding value to your customer multiplies value back to you

The goal is to benefit – ideally, to grow – the customer's business in some way. To increase the customer-perceived value of what the selling organization provides. In most cases, the seller brings their value to bear to make the machine run better, contribute meaningfully to customer success, to improve their competitive position, to capture key new opportunities.

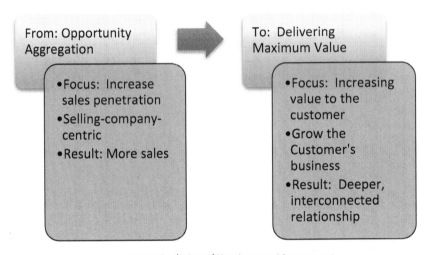

From: Opportunity Aggregation

- Focus: Increase sales penetration
- Selling-company-centric
- Result: More sales

To: Delivering Maximum Value

- Focus: Increasing value to the customer
- Grow the Customer's business
- Result: Deeper, interconnected relationship

Fig 3.5 Evolution of Key Account Management

When I talk to corporate and sales leaders about what value focus can mean when it's carried throughout the company, a few examples come to mind.

An electronic products firm was dealing with its customer, a manufacturer of test equipment for the semiconductor industry. When the customer's customer (a major microprocessor firm) shared their product roadmap for future generations of microchip, the customer was at a loss. They calculated that no circuit board materials in the world would provide the required performance. To support this customer *and their customer,* the seller embarked upon an extensive R&D project to invent suitable material in time for these customers to support their product roadmap.

When a medical imaging equipment (MRI scanner) manufacturer couldn't get their equipment to image specific areas of the body, a supplier hired engineering talent from the defense industry (expertise even the equipment manufacturer didn't have and couldn't find), then designed and built an accessory that did the job.

Unconventional Value Discovery Made Systematic

Unconventional value occurs when a buyer finds value outside of the normal box. This can be different applications for existing differentiators.

> This is an example from my wire and cable days: We had a two-step wire insulating process for one of our cables; insulation was built in two layers, usually the same color. One time, we simply fed the machine differently, with the inner and outer layers of contrasting colors to create the "wear indicator" feature, with the inner red insulation being exposed when the outer grey insulation wore through. This created value for the customer, a manufacturer of an aircraft avionics system, where reliability and failure prediction are highly sought outcomes. While our insulation material wore longer (the primary design criterion), it also introduced an unanticipated and initially not-requested value – appreciated by the airline technicians inspecting and servicing the equipment.

How do your salespeople and sellers systematically look for nonconventional value? I love telling these stories, but even more than that, I love helping clients adopt the tools to be able to repeatably and regularly create these stories for themselves...using radical value focus. When everyone in your company understands the customer's business and desired outcomes, these stories become much more commonplace.

Value Acumen Elsewhere

We'll cover these in more detail toward the end of this book, but Business Development (alliances/ecosystem), Mergers & Acquisitions, Legal, Purchasing, Manufacturing, Logistics, Channel Partners should all be keenly aware of customer value, and how they contribute to providing it.

Value Focused Companies Act, Feel and Perform Radically Differently

It should be obvious *why* a company focused on customer value will outperform average companies[19]. In this chapter, we've explored the ways that value focus and improved performance — both at the functional level and more importantly, at the organizational level — manifests all through the enterprise

---

[19] In Chapter 1, I mentioned a study which correlated "customer satisfaction" with corporate performance. Customer satisfaction measures customer perceived value on a trailing basis. I claim that this study validates value focus, but that value focus gives company's the ability to predict customer satisfaction earliery7. Eugene W. Anderson, Claes Fornell, & Sanal K. Mazvanchery. Customer Satisfaction and Shareholder Value. Journal of Marketing, October 2004. Pp 172-185

The challenge, of course, is *how* to implement value focus as an operational management routine. Cultural adoption requires simplicity and intuitiveness; it can't be perceived as an undue burden but must be seamlessly and simply integrated into the way the company operates. The rest of this book will discuss tools you'll need to take that journey.

Key Take-Aways

Corporate Leaders: It's easy for your people to claim that their processes are value focused. Claiming it isn't enough. If everyday business conversations don't discuss customer-perceived value, you are leaving money on the table. If different functions within your company aren't aware of customer value or don't all have the same answer to the question "what is our value to our customers," you have room for improvement.

Sales Leaders: Even if you have implemented "customer-focused" sales process and methodologies, there's room to take your game to the next level. A wide variety of sales training in skills and methodology take your sellers the first few steps down the path. Continuing the journey to value focus helps you prioritize opportunities, improve customer interactions, increase win rates, and forecast accuracy even further. You will need to implement a consistent coaching and management cadence around value, which could be a few simple tweaks to your existing sales methodology.

Sellers: You are the leading edge of value focus. Keeping the customer relationship to yourself is no longer an option (just think of how many other people touch that customer). If you can take advantage of everything learned by anyone else who touches your customer, you'll be more successful. It's also essential to become a student of your customer's business. If you can help a prospect make their business more successful, you will become a more trusted advisor.

Marketing Professionals: The market insights you currently gather, the content you currently compose, the competitive analysis you currently do...all benefit when performed through the lens of customer value. In combination with the aggregate marketing data you already assembled, I suggest that marketing merge that with a repository of value insights gathered from every corner of the company. Sales and/or Marketing are the natural evangelists for this repository within the company. Every tool in your arsenal is more effective when you communicate in terms of customer outcomes. Account-based marketing becomes highly focused and effective. Content becomes more impactful. Leads for sales are scored insightfully.

Product/Service Professionals: Your product/service roadmap is better informed, and there is value-based guidance to your product roadmaps. With an accurate value assessment, you can make more accurate pricing and costing projections.

CHAPTER

FOUR

Mission Critical: Radically Value Focused Customer Conversations

In the last chapter, you saw extra-silo seller roles in a company able to gather value insights. It's a radical concept, but teaching *everyone who touches a customer* about value and how to develop it increases your ability to become a mission-critical offer. Implementing radical value focus requires that you evolve beyond simple "value selling."

While there are undoubtedly more value selling methodologies and training courses out there than I will ever be able to experience, I have seen several and studied quite a few more. Some are better than others, some include things others don't, but all share a basic premise: get the prospect to understand value – their response to an outcome -- to increase the odds of a sale.

While this principle is precisely what we're going after, *radical* value conversations are different. This chapter describes the difference between value selling and radical value sales conversations. Later chapters will describe some of the tools I use with my clients to accomplish these goals.

Radical Value Focus is a Culture, Not a Training Event

First, a tale of two cultures: In my first sales job out of college, my sales manager told us to "sell the value" of our proposal; this is always great advice, but in this case, not as actionable as a sales rookie needed. Most of us tended to "tell the value," not sell it…and to confuse value with benefits. A little later, I was lucky to work in corporate culture with a relentless focus on customer value: a culture that fully operationalized "selling full value." Seeing the contrast between those environments was a true gift and set me on a journey to learn even more about the topic, to build a training and consulting practice around it, and ultimately to write this book.

To average-performing organizations, "selling value" is a sales conversation uncovering a value driver, having a customer acknowledge that your offer provides an outcome they value, and maybe share the impact that value has on their organization...rinse, repeat with new value drivers, stopping once you know they will buy when the decision team is ready. Average organizations provide salespeople with likely value drivers, and qualification questions to uncover them, and sometimes an ROI calculator tool. Above-average organizations give better tools/training to make "value conversations" more consistent and repeatable, often via sales training events, in which a role-played customer acknowledges/validates those value drivers and their impact on them.

| Match Customer Needs | Customer Acknowledges Match | Customer Describes Impact |

Probability of Winning Opportunity
→ increasing →

Fig 4.1 The Principles of Basic Value Selling. Note: the entire -critical - process of uncovering needs precedes this diagram.

Sound pretty familiar? Figure 4.1 summarizes these kinds of programs, emphasizing that the end goal is simply winning the sale. This kind of value selling falls short of what mission-critical selling requires, and that impacts your top – and bottom – line. Let's discuss a few significant areas of difference, and why they are essential in selling...but critical to an organizational focus on customer value

Sellers Should Never Settle for Understanding Approximate Value

There is a major difference in the prospect's mind between "acknowledging the value of the outcome" your offer produces for them and "quantifying the monetary impact for themselves." The level of mental engagement with the value creator/outcome is much less when you let the prospect off the hook by merely acknowledging. It's better to get the prospect to "think beyond the sale" by envisioning a payoff—*far* better still is when a seller drives the customer to a tell themselves such a detailed story that they can monetarily measure impact.

Fig 4.2 One reason for going beyond basic value selling

Psychologists and consumer choice researchers call this "the availability heuristic"[20]. It says that people give more weight to something when it is:

1. More easily recalled – more firmly carved into their memory.

2. Specific consequences surrounding a choice are more easily recalled.

3. More recently learned or processed. Tactical considerations around achieving recency in the decision process are essential.

Your offer has the most significant value when it's more vividly envisioned, recalled, and considered. Sell beyond simply envisioning consequences all the way to envisioning consequences in monetary detail (including the intermediary steps). Consequences thus become more memorable; more *available*...and therefore gain weight in a customer decision.

There are two important reasons to monetize. First, as illustrated in figure 4.2, buyers build increasingly powerful preferences for your higher-value offer. The second reason is shown in figure 4.3. If buyers don't monetize value, they can't evaluate your price as effectively (and they always seem to round down). For those selling standardized products from a price list, getting customers to monetize value can lead to reducing or avoiding discounting altogether. If you sell custom or semi-custom products, you can set optimal prices.

---

[20] Heuristic: an efficient (often imperfect) decision-making/problem-solving approach, aka: a mental shortcut. Just Google "availability heuristic" and read up on a fascinating topic. The results are all interesting, and take you to different aspects of the theory, originally described by Amos Tversky and Daniel Kahneman , which won Kahneman a Nobel Prize not long after Tversky's untimely death.

Fig 4.3 Another BIG reason for going beyond basic value selling

Since you seldom get to change your delivery costs when you drop your price, every dollar you discount comes directly out of your bottom line. Pricing your company's value is the only way to gain win-win pricing power.

Do this "what if" exercise: Take your own company's P& L statement and assume an increase in achieved prices (that is, increase your revenue line) by 1%. Since your costs don't change one bit, apply 100% of those additional funds to your before-tax income line. By what percentage did income increase?

If you could achieve revenue associated with a higher price level with the same or higher customer appreciation for your value, would you do it?

> *The idea that preference declines as price increases comes from basic theoretical economics but doesn't really appear so neatly in the real world. Only a small fraction of Americans will bother to even cross the street for a five-cent difference in gasoline prices, regardless of brand*

Unless sellers understand a customers' mental value picture, nobody in the selling company will ever understand value. Sellers can't articulate value to each other, to internal partners, or other customers. Marketing communication is less impactful, and innovators have foggier market insights to work with. Forecasts are less reliable. Leadership does not have as clear a picture with which to formulate its strategies for alliances, key accounts, complementary products, or mergers/acquisitions.

Don't Settle for Selling to Conventional Value

When your sellers use the same value points that your prospects hear from competitors, it's easy for the customer to understand. That's the good news. The bad news is that differentiation becomes limited; your sellers are not selling as much value as much as they think they are. Remember, humans decide on differences; a smaller set of differentiators is not very compelling – even before your competitors counter them. Marketing research regularly shows that price is seldom the first differentiator among products --usually the 4th or 5th. It is used when customers perceive that there is little value differential.

When sellers don't uncover value drivers thoroughly, they leave value (and money) on the table. When a customer perceives "just enough" value to decide in your favor, you are vulnerable to competitive pressure. Selling only with conventional value drivers invites trouble. Your competitors know how to blunt your normal selling points. Why make it easy for them?

When you don't uncover all value you deliver your customer, marketers have less ammunition, those responsible for innovation are forced into a me-too game, and many other functions are denied the ability to tether what they do to customer value. Leadership has a narrow field of view to formulate its strategies. The downstream effects of mediocre value focus are costly indeed.

One of the major selling behaviors I work with my clients to practice more effectively is to uncover a broader set of value drivers. I call this "uncovering unconventional value" or "learning full value," although uncovering it is hardly a costly safari into uncharted territories. We'll introduce tools to more efficiently and effectively look for unconventional value later on.

Let's be honest: the fact of the matter is that you will probably never uncover every value driver that makes up your "full value" to a customer. It's important to acknowledge that, but it's also important to strive for greatness by giving sellers tools to go looking for value. When the entire organization has tools to understand and uncover new value drivers (insert shameless pitch for chapters 9 & 10 here), the company's value culture is much stronger. For example:

> A pharmaceutical rep (who had an RN, thus, the required expertise) helped prescribing-doctors confirm that insurance submittals were in order, the outcome was fewer payment-declines and payment-delaying peer-to-peer reviews. In addition to the evident financial impact, this reduced a frustrating diversion of a doctor's time. By performing a revenue cycle management function for her clients, she created more revenue for both she and her doctor clients.

Sellers Must Uncover More Than Simple Business Value

Many value selling approaches place blinders on sellers by not incorporating *personal value* into the selling approach. I've made quite a few sales over the years by finding personal value. The thing is, I can't ever remember winning an opportunity with personal value only. A great selling methodology will discipline your salespeople to look for both.

Personal value is not always easy for non-sales functions like marketing to incorporate in their approach, but it isn't unheard of. I previously mentioned marketing departments formulating effective communications to newly appointed executives seeking to make a quick personal impact. While this use case is not a value proposition to build a company around, there is revenue to be booked by paying attention to personal gains. Here are some examples of personal value:

> The interest rate on "the only non-recourse loan with bank-like prepays and a full 25-year term" loan described at the beginning of this chapter was priced high: at about the indifference point. One proposed loan was to a family trust that had had not been updated to include the two children. When we waived the usual 1% fee (almost $80K) to change the members of the borrowing entity -- down to $1500, covering only costs of background checks and documentation, the customer's indifference to the high price was overcome.

> The seller for a medical device supplier with a new product that hadn't yet achieved Medicare approval found a doctor so impressed with the device's potential that he wanted to conduct a study on the device. Giving this physician the possibility of being published in an important journal was highly impactful customer-perceived value.

In contrast to the scope of conventional value selling approaches, sellers can uncover value which isn't corporate, but personal. These take real skill to discover, but every high-performing salesperson probably has a story like these:

> I was once told a story about Superbowl XXX; the first one played in Phoenix. The Phoenix proposal contingent put in the best proposal they could, but the stadium was sub-par, the hotel room inventory was unspectacular, etc. The only positive differentiator was that Phoenix would be "something new in the rotation" of venues. On the day that the NFL owners held the vote during their meeting (in Phoenix), the wives were limousined to a famous boutique center that catered to wealthy women. Their return from this trip was just in time for the wives to join their husbands on the final break before the vote was taken, some excitedly wearing some of their new purchases.

Make Sure Your People Understand FULL Value, Not Skipping Steps to the Win

Remember from chapter two that customers use value as a counterweight to price – specifically, the price premium. If they only perceive enough value to overcome a particular price premium, what happens if the competitor drops their price to compensate? Now, the perceived value is insufficient to win, and the seller is placed in the difficult position of trying to re-engage with a customer already in the final decision-making mode.

When sellers sell to "just enough value" rather than "full value," opportunities are at risk, pricing leverage is minimal, and the company behind the seller gets no actionable view into how they can help deliver value to the customer. It's hard to grow a profitable business on wins like this.

Selling to full value uncovers not only more value but different value – logical and emotional, business, and personal. Each single value driver for your offer often has "value tentacles" spreading throughout the customer's organization. For example, a **value network** (we'll detail these in chapter 8) associated with "reliability" looks like this:

> An electrical cable used in a piece of robotic equipment lasts longer (longer life through a larger number of robotic movement "flex cycles"). The customer's *Field Service* organization appreciates needing to make fewer repair calls. *Sales and Marketing* love being able to promote higher reliability. *Purchasing* likes the opportunity to purchase and track less spares in inventory. In this case, the customer's customer required contractually guaranteed up-time rates, with stiff penalty clauses; *Risk Management* and *Finance* were pleased to reduce the financial reserves associated with the lower risk of claims.

> This cable had other value drivers as well (chemical resistance, mechanically self-supporting), each with their own value networks: Sellers could build a group buying dynamic with supporters from all over the prospect company.

In multi-person B2B/complex buying decisions, the value associated with every one of these drivers combines additively. When we negotiated pricing for this cable, and presented the monetary value associated with each node on each value network for each value driver, the customer agreed that the value to them was the sum of all of the components.

Full Value Selling Isn't "Selling Past the Green Light"

Don't mistake selling all the value you offer for doing so at the end of an opportunity pursuit. Value development should be done throughout – as a matter of fact, developing value any time near the end of the sale becomes increasingly difficult.

The graph below illustrates this. Toward the end of a customer's buying process, building value feels like the seller is trying to talk up the price. The time to build full value in the customer's mind is well before the customer is prepared to buy.

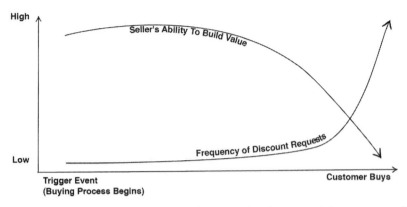

High

Seller's Ability To Build Value

Frequency of Discount Requests

Low

Trigger Event
(Buying Process Begins)

Customer Buys

Fig 4.4 Ability to build value (resist discounting) vs. frequency of discount requests[21]

In fact, as figure 4.4 also shows, customers most frequently request discounts after they have decided on an offer's value.

Don't Stop at a Training Event: Make Sure That You Coach and Instill Behavior Change

This doesn't apply to value selling programs in particular, but any training program without a very solid coaching and sustainment plan is a doomed investment.

Any training (sales or otherwise) without coaching and sustainment is fine when the training content requires only "knowledge transfer." Knowledge transfer content includes how to enter an order, produce a bid, operate the phone system...that sort of thing. A lot of sales training, including selling to full value, is a *learned behavior*, and behavior change doesn't happen (for other than a few exceptional performers) by virtue of a single training event (or by just reading this book, unfortunately).

Without robust sustainment, the typical failure mode is a rapid loss of momentum, followed by a reversion to prior methods. The company benefits only during the brief period of inexperienced practice, and future initiatives bear the burden of lost management credibility – it gets harder each time you try.

---

[21] This diagram was born during a fascinating conversation with Rich Blakeman, whose book on Channel management is quoted elsewhere. I don't feel right publishing it without thanking him for that, and many other enlightening talks.

Develop a System to Capture Value Insights for Use Throughout Your Enterprise

Previously, we detailed the stark difference between normal organizations and value-focused organizations in their understanding of how their products and services deliver value to a customer, and how to engage every part of the company in doing so.

To instill a sales culture of customer value, you need intuitive, simple, and easily coached. If you're trying to build a company-wide value culture, simplicity becomes vital.

While many value selling approaches have one or more of the above, I've not seen one that has all of them. That's part of why you're reading this book.

Value focus has much of its value outside of the selling organization, and the selling organization needs to use a common language with the rest of the company.

The selling organization needs to search for all of the value drivers, not just the usual suspects.

Sellers need to fully engage the client in monetizing each value component. This tethers value to price.

Key Take-Aways

Corporate Leaders: This chapter primarily covers how value conversations take place. It would be easy to assume that this kind of conversation is confined to the sales organization. Nothing could be further from the truth. The types of sales conversations we discuss in this chapter can – and should – be conducted by anyone who touches the customer. As a leader, it falls to you to insist on the adoption of value focus company-wide. I hope this chapter helped you define what you should look for more carefully.

Also, I hope the discussion of sales coaching and sustainment impacted your perception of those kinds of training that require behavior change (in contrast to training for simple knowledge transfer). Question any sales training initiative that doesn't include a coaching and sustainment component.

Sales Leaders: Even if you have implemented "value selling" sales process and methodologies, there's room to take your game to the next level. Continuing the journey to *full value* (fully developed value from all differentiators) focus helps you prioritize opportunities, improve customer interactions, increase win rates, and forecast accuracy. You will need to implement a consistent coaching and management cadence around value, which could be a few simple tweaks to your existing sales methodology...to adding my Full Value Selling®

methodology into your management cadence...to installing process and methodology if you don't have either.

Sales Enablement Leaders: World-class selling organizations are filled with sellers who can develop full value. As you are building a sales system, playbooks, and methodology, make sure that you build a sales enablement journey to build and sustain such an organization.

Sales Operations Leaders: Sales metrics need to encourage sellers to engage prospects in value articulation. I've seen value-focused insights in opportunity pursuits, and you need to make sure your system is capable of gathering, measuring, and tracking value – as uncovered by sellers.

Leaders of all functions who come in contact with customers: I hope this chapter opened your eyes to what conversations with customers should uncover. Training your teams to have these conversations is relatively straightforward, but coaching to establish consistently productive conversations will take commitment.

Sellers: If you know how to have value-focused conversations, you will be more successful. Also, if you can take advantage of everything learned by anyone else who touches your customer, you'll be more successful. As you become a student of your customer's business—and fix their value gaps with your offer, you'll become a trusted resource. Once you can help a prospect make their business more successful, you will become a trusted advisor. Become a student of your customer's business.

Marketing Professionals: Developing a joint vision with sales on what value impacts are the most compelling with your customers doesn't mean "giving ground" to sales. It involves placing customer value at the center of what you each do.

Product/Service Professionals: As you engage with how customers value your products, you innovate more efficiently and effectively. If you learn to speak the language of customer value inside the company, and learn how to discuss perceived value with customers, you are building key bridges to a more productive organization.

PART
THREE

To Know Thy Customer's Business, Ye Must Know Business

Who do you trust for medical advice: Your doctor, or a pharmaceutical sales rep? The answer is obvious, but the reason is because a doctor understands your body as a whole system, learns your medical history and labs before diagnosing. The pharma rep, on the other hand, knows a lot about how one (or a few) drug(s) works on one disease. Similarly, sellers *who aspire to developing maximum value need broad business acumen* rather than merely product expertise.

Learn Your Customer's Ecosystem, and Their Place In it

The value training we talked about in the last chapter requires generalized business acumen. Sellers need to understand your customer's world holistically: their business environment, competitive landscape, what the opportunities company is (or isn't) pursuing or wants to pursue, what challenges they face, what resources they have, what resources they lack, and so forth. While a basic SWOT[22] analysis can be a foundational tool, it seldom provides sufficient insight to be able to uncover new value consistently.

To become a valued resource, sellers must demonstrate value to customers at every contact. This chapter describes foundational business acumen. Your sellers, everyone who contacts a customer during the entire arc of their

---

[22] A listing of Strengths, Weaknesses, Opportunities, and Threats. I find doing SWOT analysis with sales teams is great for getting them into the proper mindset and gives a summary overview, but doesn't often produce high-quality insights. SWOTT, which adds Trends, is better, but still not up to the task.

experience with your company, should all be conversant. We'll discuss some tools developed by famous consultants & academics, augmented by some of my own.

Different companies will use the material in Part 3 differently. Some companies call on one, or a small number of industries (If you sell paper-making machinery, your customer universe is finite and known). Other companies (say, commercial banks) are at the other end of the spectrum: Each new opportunity requires their sellers to learn a new industry in significant detail. How a company develops business acumen in their organization will be shaped by this, plus a few other factors. As you read these chapters, consider the best ways to operationalize these tools.

Here in part 3, we will discuss your customer's business environment (yours too, of course). Companies are shaped by their environments: their industries, and their competitive landscape. As salespeople search for customer-perceived value, they should understand how each customer experiences their own world. This means first understanding a customer's industry, then understanding how they compete in it.

The world's great business schools have provided sales professionals with some great tools. Harvard Business School's Michael Porter has given us some great ones, which I incorporate into the Business Profile tool describe in the following chapter. I would be remiss if I didn't give him due.

The Seven Forces Model: The Major Forces that Shape a Company

Harvard Business School's Michael Porter's gift to the world is reducing complex systems into simple frameworks that help the rest of us work more efficiently. One of the models he introduced was his 1979 "Five Forces" model [23], which describes the major factors influencing an industry and competition within that industry.

Others have built on Porter's Five Forces work, adding a couple more forces. *I give tools to help my clients expand the analysis of the customer, the central circle in the figure.* The additions are useful for building our understanding of how customers perceive their own competitive environment. All of these find their way into the Business Profile you will see in chapter 5.

---

[23] There are lots of articles etc. on the five forces model. Several point you back to a couple associated with Harvard Business School, where Michael Porter has become an icon; quick explainer video first: https://hbr.org/video/3590615226001/the-explainer-porters-five-forces
http://www.isc.hbs.edu/strategy/business-strategy/Pages/the-five-forces.aspx

The forces model is built on the idea that a company is shaped by its environment, and that several major forces do almost all of the shaping. The model appears below.

Figure P3.1 The Seven Forces Model. Significant Contributors: Michael Porter

We'll go into depth on more than just the seven forces in the coming chapter, so I won't describe them here. This analytic framework is an excellent foundation for the kind of business acumen that professional sellers (any great employee, for that matter) need. I borrow from it so heavily that I wanted to credit the sources in more than a footnote.

CHAPTER
FIVE

Efficiently Becoming an Expert in Your Customer's Business

A seller becomes a trusted advisor when a customer believes they build value *beyond what they get elsewhere (differences,* remember?). In the sales training industry, you'll hear this additional value called perspective, insight, challenging, and more.

To be elevated by customers to "trusted advisor" status, customer-facing professionals must *consistently* uncover novel, or *unexpected* (to the customer, that is) perspectives for their customers; the ability to get them to think about their own business in new ways. Your people must know more about your customer's business than competitors, and in ways your prospect hasn't considered.

> *I've been challenged on this by an interesting point: what if there is only one seller who provides an insight already known to the customer? This would undoubtedly elevate that seller's credibility above other sellers, but I don't know that it would position them as a trusted advisor.*

The foundation of systematically being able to uncover value, even in unconventional spots, is business acumen. Selling to a business means helping that customer become more successful or profitable in one or more ways. This requires sellers to build some basic business savvy.

The figure below overviews the elements of business acumen in the left two columns then gives a "starter list" of some of the business outcomes your business analysis can suggest.

Your Customer's World

External Forces	Internal Forces	Potential Outcomes (Goal: Desired Outcomes)

Figure 5.1. Business acumen (the two left sections) suggest business outcomes often unanticipated by the customer.

You will see the six of the seven forces model I described in the introduction to Part 3. These are the forces in the prospect's business environment that shape their world and outlook. The center section expands the "target company" analysis into six major shaping factors. If your company sells into a single vertical market or industry, some of these factors may be consistent across your entire customer base, but they are still essential factors shaping your prospect's world view.

The right section illustrates many – not all – of the outcomes your offer might be able to help a prospect achieve. Seeking a broad sweep of outcomes is important for sellers. Many prospects evaluate a potential purchase with blinders on; very commonly, prospects take a silo-limited view of their situation and of the problem they are trying to solve for. As you look at these possible outcomes for your product or service, notice how many of them are outside of the limits of your typical customer's thought process.

Marketing and product functions play a significant role in describing typical value for broad homogeneous customer groups and preparing sellers to uncover predicted value. Many sales organizations, though, have a couple of top people who regularly find "off-the-predicted-path" value. Having just a few such stars is not good enough. I want you to build a company full of such trusted advisors. This requires a purposely built, organization-wide competence: a framework to help sellers grasp the entire "lay of the land," the "value landscape" of a target. I call the framework for mapping out this landscape the **Business Profile.**

Sellers certainly need the big picture insights gained from financial statements and external sources, but a detailed business profile requires more. Sellers need a tool that enables them to *spot pockets of achievable value*. If you aspire to become a trusted resource to a customer, you must become deeply familiar with their business. In this chapter, we'll describe the depth of knowledge required to produce "trusted advisor" insights.

The Business Profile: A Value Discovery Canvas

The business profile tool is one that organizes key information from financial statements and other public resources, combined with direct questioning.

The Business Profile is a simple yet comprehensive scan of the major value-producing parts of a target company. It gives a holistic summary view, helping sellers see how their target company is a network of inter-related parts, with key leverage points for creating value. It provides the selling organization a canvas on which to create a thorough, efficient value discovery plan.

The profile is easy to absorb and gives everyone in your company the same view of the essentials of your customer's business. Using the profile, it's easier for contributors from all over your company to uncover possible value creation for your customers.

Completing a profile on a target firm is often a collaborative effort.

- Marketing professionals often have the research skills to gather a great deal of information, especially from public companies. It's also easy for them to build a template business profile for a typical company in a target market – which can be refined and "personalized" for each specific target.

- Sales, as the primary interface to the customer, can often provide key details specific to many of these areas, and they are a great guideline for in-depth discovery work. Every seller role, though, should provide their unique perspective.

- Product experts (engineering, product design, development, underwriting, etc.) can often provide eye-opening perspectives based upon their specialized customer interactions.

- Customer service, billing, accounts receivable...any role that touches the customer often has knowledge that enriches the breadth and depth of the profiling exercise.

Elements of the Business Profile

Let's examine the business profile sections described in figure 5.1. Rather than following the order shown there, this section progresses with some big picture views, then progresses into some of the more narrowly focused aspects of the profile. You will end up with an insightful picture of a target company's business, and some creative potential value insights.

1. Key Trends in the Company's Business Environment

A company is a product of its environment every bit as much they are the sum of their decisions and actions. You can't really understand your customers until you understand the bigger world in which they live. A great place to start looking for a public company is the *management's discussion* in financial statements or *investor presentations.* Did they mention any challenges in/with:

- Their markets? How are their markets changing, and how is it impacting the company?

- Technology? Are any technology trends emerging as threats, opportunities, or both? Are any technology trends allowing new competitors to enter the market?

What about analyst reports? Whether public or privately held, are there any hints in trade publications, press releases, or news stories? Can you infer anything from their advertising or promotional material? Do they have a publicly held competitor who lives in the same market/regulatory environment? Many of these external trends are discoverable before even contacting a prospect, and your knowing them in advance helps build a lot of credibility.

Regulation can either be an opportunity or a threat, but it is an ever-present component of any company's business environment. The business profile should outline significant aspects and trends in the regulatory environment. There is a great deal of truth to the claim that government regulation affects all competitors equally, but I would argue that it is true only when all competitors "look the same" to a government entity[24]. Regulation doesn't always affect all competitors similarly, and there is value to be uncovered for the supplier that understands those differences.

- Government regulations. Are regulations increasing? More important, are regulations affecting all competitors symmetrically? Do regulations incentivize certain competitive behaviors? Are any competitors noticeably more regulation-friendly than the norm?

---

[24] See Uber vs. traditional taxi service in any number of cities worldwide.

Regulation will also always be a moving target for as long as there are humans elected to office to change regulation in one way or another; thus, there is value to be uncovered by those with the competency to understand new regulations and help their customers adapt and comply more rapidly.

2. Competitors

How do your customer's *competitors* compete with each other? Do they pursue the same strategy (or value discipline, see section 3 below)? What advantages do they have relative to one another, and how does that manifest in the competitive dynamic. Which competitors do a particular customer worry about? Which do they confront most directly? The answers to these questions should inform a great deal of value-hunting for not only your salespeople but for your entire customer-value-focused company.

When analyzing your customer's competitive environment, look at each major competitor's value discipline, at the seller/customer matrix below:

2b. Substitutes

We often lose sight of the ways our customers could satisfy the need (could get an adequate outcome) using not-in-kind competitors. Trucking firms could compete with rail, ship, pipelines, or even locally-sourcing of a commodity, for instance. Your customers lose sight of this same thing. Part of the value we can bring to our customers is awareness of substitutes so that we can help them mitigate a leakage of customers to not-in kind competition. Some customers may simply decide they can do the job in-house as well as a vendor can.

Surgery is a substitute for some pharmaceuticals. Remodeling is a substitute for a new house. In a very real sense, substitutes are simply a type of competitor, which is why they overlap in the seven forces diagram. Because people often let "competitor myopia" cause them to overlook substitutes, I like to call this competitor type out explicitly.

Be aware of "substitute tunnel vision." I recall being told that once upon a time, the product managers of Gatorade said to themselves that they were by far the #1 product in their market, which they defined as something like "Citrus flavored electrolyte drinks whose performance has been validated by exercise physiologists." Clearly, this self-definition was a purposeful effort to ignore substitutes. There's an obvious risk in looking in your world like this. As a potential supplier, helping customers doing this same thing re-frame their worldview might pay huge dividends.

Any new entrants? The world is littered with the graves of companies who failed to see how new entrants would displace them[25]. Companies, including your customers, can often fail to see new entrants as a threat. Helping your customers spot new entrants might enable you to realize value by helping them deal more effectively. You might also be able to either take advantage (to align with a new entrant) or insulate yourself from the harm of the new entrant. There is some self-interest in here too: remember, for every company who failed to see a new market entrant, there are many suppliers who cast their lot with a doomed customer.

> In the early 1980s, a company named Kroy owned the desktop publishing market with office machines that printed various type sizes and styles on clear tape (the tape's outline disappeared when photocopied – try this with Scotch® brand tape if you want to see for yourself). Users would print documents on an impact printer with spaces instead of section headings or headlines, then tape the nicely printed headings in place, then photocopy those originals. Kroy rejected advances by makers of computers and laser printers – who wanted to utilize their dominant distribution in the office supply industries. These new entrants created a superior substitute for the old lettering machine.

3. What is the Company Strategy/Value Discipline

It's good basic information to know who a customer's competitors are. It's far more insightful to understand how those companies interact competitively. That is, what differentiated value do *they* try to produce for *their customers?* Competitors seldom try to compete head-to-head. If you know how a company competes, you should be able to more closely align with their priorities.

> *When competitors don't compete head-to-head but try to differentiate themselves, they are trying to get themselves off the demand curve taught in economics classes –the ones that assume that products are entirely replaceable commodities. When they succeed, they can achieve outcomes –like, say, premium pricing – that are impossible in the mathematical world of supply/demand economics. If you know any company that gets away with premium pricing, you know that the economic "rule" that increased price drives decreased demand is less valuable than your econ teacher was letting on.*

The first element of the business profile is how your customer has decided to compete for business. How do they provide value to *their* customers?

---

[25] see Video, Blockbuster. Also see Honda motorcycles, who entered that market at the very small end, migrating their product offering upward.

Michael Treacy and Fred Wiersema reduced all of the competitive strategies companies pursue down to three "Value Disciplines."[26] If you know how your customer intends to create value with their customers – that is, what types of value they try to create for their customers, you will have a much better path to helping them create more of the same.

Treacy and Wiersema describe three generic value disciplines, which drive many strategy and implementation issues. I will outline them briefly, but their work is important enough for any business leader to invest the time in their book.

Operational Excellence is the **first** value discipline. It means "providing customers with reliable products or services at competitive prices and delivered with minimal difficulty or inconvenience[27]. These companies are maniacal about cost-cutting, process simplification, logistical efficiency, etc. One does not often find products with industry-leading performance and features unless those features are about delivering efficiency or convenience. Amazon's automatic reorder services and devices are an innovative front end to an operational effectiveness business model.

Customer Focus is the **second** value discipline, where companies "continually tailor and shape products and services to fit an increasingly fine definition of the customer.[28]" "Increasingly fine" does not necessarily mean "increasingly small"; customer-focused companies aren't necessarily single-niche players. Mass customization is used heavily by customer-focused players to efficiently provide a custom-fit offer to multiple industries: A flexible platform with lots of easy adjustments to produce a very custom-feeling product/service for a variety of different customers. Other characteristics of customer focus: decentralized marketing, empowered salespeople, to fine-tune offers for specific customers easily and efficiently. Long-term customer relationships are the goal, and customer-focused companies will often spend time looking at metrics such as lifetime customer value and the like. I've worked in and with many customer-focused companies with all or most of these characteristics – some in services, and some in manufactured products.

Product Leadership is the **third** value discipline. Treacy and Wiersema's HBR article sums it up best: "Companies that pursue… product leadership strive to produce a continuous stream of state-of-the-art products and services. Reaching

---

[26] Treacy and Wiersema's work is summarized in a Harvard Business Review article. https://hbr.org/1993/01/customer-intimacy-and-other-value-disciplines. Or if you want even more detail, read their book The Discipline of Market Leaders, a read I *highly* recommend.

[27] Ibid.

[28] ibid.

that goal requires them to challenge themselves in three ways. First, they must be creative. More than anything else, being creative means recognizing and embracing ideas that usually originate outside the company. Second, product leadership companies must commercialize their ideas quickly. To do so, all their business and management processes have to be engineered for speed. Third and most important, product leaders must relentlessly pursue new solutions to the problems that their own latest product or service has just solved. If anyone is going to render their technology obsolete, they prefer to do it themselves[29]" Here's an example: Netflix replaced Blockbuster's video rental business model with video rental-via-mail, then replaced themselves with video-on-demand.

Think of the three disciplines as a three-dimensional space. A company choosing one dimension works to be superior (to competitors) on that axis. On the other two axes, competitive and other forces drive a "minimum acceptable performance level"; no company can survive by mastering one and abandoning either of the other two. The "focus" value discipline chosen, plus the "table stakes" level of the other two disciplines, describes that company's current competitive direction.

Figure 5.2 Treacy and Wiersema's Three Value Disciplines as a three-dimensional shape

Let's look at the smartphone industry to illustrate a highly competitive industry where the three value disciplines are demonstrated. HTC (no longer a major player, but still a great pure example) pursues a value discipline of operational excellence, while Samsung is about product leadership, and Apple positions its simple user environment/user experience on a customer intimacy axis.

The smartphone example illustrates the market-defined minimum expectation on all three dimensions. HTC needs to meet a high minimum of feature

---

[29] ibid

functionality and ease-of-use to be a viable player. Similarly, Apple does not need to always be the first to market with any given feature (like water-resistance, to my great frustration), but does need to keep pace at some level on the market expected minimums on functionality and cost-effectiveness.

What does this mean for a value-focused supplier? Imagine you want to sell your company's glass displays to each of these three. Don't you think that you want to sell different outcomes...different value – and possibly different versions of your product to each? I might want to:

- Sell one company the latest/greatest in drop resistance and lumens/watt (brightness units while extending battery life),

- Approach the second competitor with the lowest manufactured cost (logistical and manufacturability outcomes, maybe the last generation of display at a lower cost),

- Seek out the product designers at the third company to see how your glass can enable their latest design concept or to see how you can collaboratively dream up even greater new user experiences.

Conversely, if you sold exactly the same outcome to each customer with the same value proposition, would you be seen as a trusted, collaborative partner?

4. What are Senior Management's Top Priorities?

Public companies often announce some management priorities or at least discuss them during earnings calls. Whenever a C-level executive promises something or describes and initiative to his stock analysts and investors, it has a way of becoming a priority for the entire organization.

I think it's unforgivable to walk into a prospective customer without knowing what was discussed/promised in either of these forums. If any executives have been interviewed or profiled in trade publications, make sure you discover and read those as well.

The business profile should record any key initiatives, growth plans, strategies, including acquisition strategies and appetites. Especially important (so important that they get their own section in the business profile) are...

5. Major Risks Faced by the Company

Management will disclose some of these when talking about significant priorities, but it's common for management only to discuss obvious risks on investor presentations. You may have to do some digging to get more than that. Talking with vendors, customers, and industry analysts can reveal new perspectives about the business environment and dangerous trends.

Unacknowledged risks are supremely important. Displaying the insight to discuss these openly (as appropriate, and with your best bedside manner) can uncover critical value gaps. Another major area to show your value: the risks they don't know about. Your sellers will often have helped another customer with a risk that this one doesn't even know about yet. If they can be alerted to – and then acknowledge, envision, and value that risk, it can be the source of significant value.

Risks can come in the form of competitive, regulatory, markets, or risks of being replaced or displaced.

6. Key Processes/Activities

In this section, the business profiler should broadly look at the prospect company as a network of interconnected processes. While it's useful to know about all major process and activity flows within a company, the business profile should identify and describe those which are unique to a company and key activities/processes which it uses to distinguish itself in its market.

For example, a company that provides a lot of custom or semi-custom products/services is likely to consider their design and/or application engineering process as a strategic differentiator, as well as how efficiently they can breakdown/set up or turn over between customers. Heavily engineered product companies and professional services companies depend on the success of recruiting and retention processes.

Describe any manufacturing, underwriting, consulting, development, customer intake, customer handoff (execution/delivery), software coding (do they use one of the lean methodologies, or are they a traditional shop?). If such a customer has a process for screening new business ideas and approving business cases, learn about it, and outline it in the business profile. Consider how these processes might differ for firms pursuing product leadership, customer intimacy, or operational excellence value disciplines.

Some processes are common to all companies, like payroll, hiring, accounting, etc. It's good practice to think through these to see if they are relevant to your offer. If so, try to expand your knowledge of those.

Key process/activity analysis is a key part of the business profile. Many sellers' products and services impact a customer's process (or processes) or activities. Hopefully, the impact provides improved outcomes -- plural. Far too many selling organizations get tunnel vision, looking only at the "primary target process" and mirror the same outcomes every competitor promotes. The reason this section is so important is that it helps you, your sellers, and your entire company broaden their view of possible customer impacts (customer value) that you can target.

7. Key Resources/Inputs

Next, look at how those processes are fed. Another way to look at a target company is as a black box: a machine (collection of processes) that produces profits and happy customers, *consuming various inputs*. Software companies, for instance, require skilled software engineers and coders. Other companies require specialized people skills of other types. These would be key resources to note on such a company's business profile.

> In addition to people, companies can require specific commodities and supply relationships. The inventor of SoftSoap® lengthened his first-mover advantage in the new-to-the-world (in the consumer space, at least) liquid soap market by locking up the entire world's supply of a critical packaging component--the liquid soap pump dispenser tops (at the time there were only a couple of producers) -- for a year or so to preserve their market position. How would you like to have been one of those salesmen that year?

Other key resources are intellectual property: patents, copyrights, trademarks, trade secrets, process know-how, and the like.

If you can improve your prospect company's ability to obtain or retain key resources – even tangentially – you can uncover significant value.

One key resource is you. To your customer, you are a supplier. Key suppliers can shape customers' industries[30]. If your customer competes for some scarce resource, you should know about it. The same goes for commodities they purchase (I'll talk more about dysfunctional purchasing behavior later). Understanding your customer's relationship with their other suppliers will give you valuable insights about how they might desire to have the relationship with you look like.

Thomas Williams and Thomas Saine have published a great, <u>The Seller's Challenge</u>. Chapter nine of that book focuses on key details in the customer/supplier relationship. There's so much great information in that chapter (the whole book, if you're a seller) that I can recommend it without reservation. One concept they present is a model of the supplier/purchaser relationship – it helps sellers understand where they currently sit with a customer and possible strategies for success.

---

[30] I recommend the book <u>Growth Partnering, How to Build Your Company's Profits by Building Customer Profits</u>, by Mack Hanan copyright 1992 AMACOM, a division of the American Management Association.

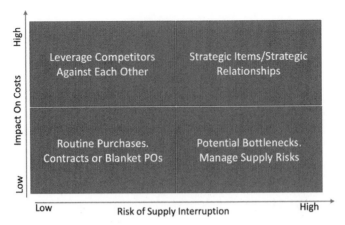

Figure 5.3 The Seller/customer relationship matrix. The Kraljic Matrix, adapted by Van Weele, Williams, and Saine

In their model, there are two dimensions:

1. How significant is the cost impact of the product or service? If the cost is a small impact on the total bill of materials, or if an offer doesn't impact other costs significantly, that offer will be on the bottom half of the matrix. Examination gloves are a small cost impact for a hospital, for instance.

2. How significant is the supply risk? Is this a long lead-time item, or if there are few or one supplier of the product/service, an interruption in supply is critical. SoftSoap purchased the entire world's supply of pump tops to prolong its first-mover advantage in the liquid soap category.

How those two dimensions combine yields a two-by-two matrix. Each quadrant of the matrix guides the sourcing/procurement function to a supplier strategy[31].

Understanding how your customer looks at you and your product category should be a crucial part of your business profile.

8. Key Partners

Commercial alliances and complementary products are becoming a more prominent feature in many industries, and these relationships take many forms. The business profile should capture these relationships to get a more complete picture of the prospective customer's business.

Complementary products and ecosystem partners are becoming more important all the time. Some technology products have sensitized many companies to the

---

[31] The Seller's Challenge, Thomas Williams and Thomas Saine. Copyright 2018. Chapter 9.

ability to have a partner add value to what they offer. A cellular phone service is more valuable when it provides international roaming through partnership agreements with foreign carriers. That carrier's service is also more valuable when there are a large variety of handsets to fit a large number of user profiles. Smartphones' value is largely in the ability to "personalize" your device via apps, and the thousands of available apps create a highly personalized experience. Some companies proactively create ecosystems of complementary products to create synergistic value for their users. Technology companies weren't pioneers in creating ecosystems: retailers with complementary – even competing -- goods have congregated in single geographic areas for thousands of years. Recognizing or even envisioning networks of complementary ecosystem partners can uncover powerful value for customers.

> *A common example: many towns see auto dealers, furniture retailers, and other types of business in geographic clusters. An unsavory example: Skid Row. In 1850s Seattle (or Vancouver, depending on whose history you read), gambling halls, saloons, brothels, flop-houses, etc. set up a complementary service offering by locating near one another that none of the individual businesses provided on their own.*

Helping your customers create ecosystems--or understand when they are already part of one -- can be a game-changer too. Key suppliers can sell products, license patents, supply know-how, and more. If the prospect has already formed important relationships with other suppliers, use that as evidence that they are open to partnering with suppliers. Alliances are commonplace with suppliers of complementary products/services, ecosystem members, and referral partners.

9. Customers

A key part of the business profile analysis is the study of your customer's customers. They are almost surely the most important influence on your customers. Being able to provide help and insight for your customers to help them sell more is a tremendous value-added for them. Can you answer these questions about your customers' customers?

- Can you characterize your customer's market and the concentration (percent of the total sales revenue from the major suppliers)? Is the market fragmented? Are there easily winnable chunks of market share? Or, are they dominant in their market, and want to grow by expanding their sales to existing customers?

- What new customers would your customers like to win? Do they have plans to enter new markets?

- What is their customer churn rate – how many existing customers are they losing compared to new customer acquisition? Why are the trends the way they are, and how can you help improve them?

- What does your customer's ideal customer look like, and what value are they looking for?

- What value discipline is your customer using to differentiate themselves with their customers…and how can you help?

- What does the post-sale implementation, service, cross-sell and up-sell environment (and revenue streams) look like?

Your customer's world is shaped by their customers. Value-focused companies make the customer's customers an integral part of how the value they provide.

> Boeing spends vast resources designing its aircraft for airline passengers. They have deep insight into lighting (colors, intensity, diffusion, reading lights vs. cabin lights, etc.), environmental (filtration, temperature, pressure, velocity, humidity, and far more), perceived space (whether the cabin feels more spacious with the widest point at the shoulder or eye level), seating (how to make you more comfortable in less actual space), overhead bins (capacity, perceived headroom while closed, intuitive operation, ease of loading/unloading), windows (bigger, self-darkening, etc.), and more that I'm sure I can't even imagine. That's a lot of time, money, and expertise invested in people who don't buy airplanes.

While we talk about it quite a bit throughout this book, it's insufficient to simply make sure you know *what* a customer wants to buy. Sellers should also know *how* those customers want to buy, where they want to buy, how often, what time…and, most importantly of all, *why* they want to buy. If a sales and market coverage strategy is out of alignment with those, a client might still be leaking revenue. You can best help them realize better outcomes by gaining a clear picture of their markets and customers.

Look at Section 8 (key resources/inputs) again. Your customer's customer thinks of *your customer* as a supplier. Your customer is subject to the same dynamics with their customers. Those dynamics are entirely independent of the dynamic you have with your customer. Start by understanding the customer/supplier relationship through that lens.

9B. Revenue Streams

Some companies have a relatively simple set of revenue streams. Nonetheless, it's important to understand all revenue streams and how they relate to each other.

When profiling a customer, look at their revenues from sales, rentals, leasing, financing income, service contracts, design services, disposal/recycling, licensing, revenue sharing with complementary providers, and so on. Catalog whatever income streams a customer has. Then try to determine which you might be able to affect.

Also, characterize each revenue with respect to size, profitability, whether they are managed for profitability, customer relationship, or some other goal. Some revenue streams are money losers; a customer is sometimes looking for a way out of one of these...or some way to replace it.

In addition to existing relationships, try to find out if any revenue streams are planned or desired. Many companies, especially those in technology, are trying to shift their revenue streams. A big trend right now is to convert software sales to subscription-based software-as-a-service (SaaS). The desire to add or shift revenue streams can be a significant value creation opportunity if you can help them accomplish that outcome.

10. Channels

Any way of getting your product or service to your ultimate end-user is an indirect channel. Reps, distributors, value-added resellers, brokers, et cetera are examples, and if your customer prefers to buy through such suppliers, suppliers need to work through the channel partners the customer wants to buy from.

The business profile should spell out the relationships the prospect has with their channel: existing, future, areas of dissatisfaction. Describe or diagram the major channel relationships and map the influences and parties between supplier and end-user.

A significant influence in my professional growth, Rich Blakeman, asserts[32], companies need to coordinate direct and indirect sellers to ensure that they complement rather than cannibalize. As you profile any business, see if they are accomplishing that goal.

> I once had a client who had signed an agreement with one of the nation's largest medical equipment distributors, paying them a distributor's margin to achieve greater market coverage. Two years into the agreement, my client determined that their own sales force had uncovered over 97% of won opportunities on their own – and had performed the vast bulk of the selling work to boot. The distributor had clearly not provided the value they were being compensated for.

Your business profile should describe the relationships and highlight any potential channel conflicts – these represent potential value gaps.

---

[32] The Hybrid Sales Channel. How to Ignite Growth by Bridging the Gap between Direct and Indirect Sales, Copyright 2016 by Rich Blakeman McGraw-Hill.

11. Value Proposition(s)

While it would be nice if a company's value proposition aligned perfectly with their value discipline/company strategy, the business profiling exercise should examine and highlight any disconnects – a great area to explore for value.

The value proposition is the proposed value that a company uses to position an offer in an initial approach: this might appear in marketing materials and/or to gain interest in allowing a salesperson to begin a discovery process. This part of the profile expands on – and should dovetail with -- the customer's strategy/value discipline. What value do their products and/or services propose to their customers? How well are those proposition(s) received by customers (and how can you find out)? Do you see any opportunities for adjustment?

How does your customer differentiate themselves throughout the selling process? Is differentiation-- how the prospect's offer is differentiated in the customer's mind *at the time of purchase* – the same as it was proposed at the outset? Is that OK? Is any change a planned one? How differentiation aligns (or doesn't) with the value proposition is a source of stimulating conversation in my business, but also for many companies trying to find potential sources of value with a customer.

> It's common for a VP of Sales who engaged us in a sales performance path to comment that "establishing a common selling language" was one of the most valuable aspects of our engagement. This was in contrast to their thoughts when we were still in the exploration stage: they thought "common language" was a frivolous claim. As a result, this is one of those value points that isn't in the original value proposition unless the customer asks for it.

Other differentiation aspects you should explore and understand include: Do they serve different markets that highlight distinct differentiators? Are their differentiators a fit for any unaddressed markets? Would some additional differentiation help, and how could they execute on that?

Pricing strategy is a part of the value proposition because, in the mind, price declares value. Identify whether a company is a premium product, a price-driven alternative, or a pseudo-premium product (advertises as premium, but discounts to win bids when all is said and done). *Discounting behavior* by the customer tells a story all its own. I always want to find out how heavily discounting plays a part in each revenue stream; are any revenue streams more susceptible to discounting than others? Is discounting concentrated in any regions, territories, customers, and/or salespeople? How does any discounting affect, change, or damage the customer's perceived differentiation?

Can you learn the customer's product innovation plan, such as product roadmaps, product development pipeline, or acquisition strategies? In addition to outlining the process they use to screen ideas (in the process section of the profile), outline the projects and concepts in development. Also, see what you can learn about the challenges being encountered in those projects.

12. The Company's Cost Structure

The cost structure/breakeven analysis of your prospect should be summarized in this area of the business profile. I maintain that there is little benefit to sellers in being able to perform a detailed financial ratio analysis on a company's financial statements (except for specific industries). A sales professional should *know how to* perform a cost structure analysis, though: translating formal financial reports into a cost structure analysis.

Identify the major fixed and variable costs the company incurs. With minimal training, people can be shown where to find major variable costs (in cost of goods sold, for instance), fixed expenses (G&A is an example), and fixed asset costs (fixed assets on the balance sheet, plus depreciation expense on the income statement). Rather than describing it in detail here, I encourage those you learn more about in chapter 6, immediately following this chapter.

Where is the company with respect to their breakeven point? Are there any major cost leakages known by you, your sellers, industry experts, or their management? Does management perceive any areas for improvement? Describe your findings in this part of the business profile.

Everyone in your organization, especially customer-facing sellers, should have a basic understanding of breakeven analysis, and it's definitely something they should have the acumen to read – and to be able to produce insights from. Many companies, though, will find it useful to offload the bulk of this analysis to sales support or financial colleagues.

The key here: It's more important for most people to analyze financial statements to determine *operational health* than it is to do detailed financial analysis – which is meant to measure financial health, not the primary value gap your sellers are looking for.

The Why of the Business Profile: Understanding Potential Customer Value

Remember that value is the desirability of one or more outcomes. A customer can't desire something until they perceive it, then believe it. The reason to become an expert in a customer's business is to build value in the form of additional outcomes.

The right section of figure 5.1 describes some of the outcomes your offer might be able to deliver for a customer.

Also remember, value only exists in a customer's mind. The business profile helps us look at the customer's world through the customer's eyes...but without the customer's blinders. As sellers, we need to uncover novel outcomes and novel ways for a prospective customer to achieve a valued result.

If you are a leader putting your company on a path toward a radically value focused culture, you need two things:

1. Customer insight, not just customer knowledge

2. Solution expertise (ability to express product/service knowledge in the form of customer results) applied insightfully to a customer's situation to uncover new value.

Any differentiation you have doesn't turn into value until it "makes a landing" in a customer's mind and connects to a customer-desired outcome. The more outcomes you can produce for a customer, the more value you have. The more value your customer *believes* you will produce in the future, the higher your perceived value. Selling organizations often leave value on the table by not understanding their customer's business intimately enough.

Knowing Thy Customer's Business

If you complete this customer profiling exercise, you will develop an outstanding insight into what that customer's world looks like and what their aspirations are. That insight will help you to generate a lot of value-triggering ideas.

This value-searching profile is pretty exhaustive. I seldom hear someone complain that they knew their customer too well, though...or that even though a competitor knew more about your customer, everything turned out fine anyway. My experience in finding unconventional value is that knowing the entire lay of the land is critical to finding new ways for customers to experience value.

One note on efficiency: Sections that are industry-wide can be cloned from one company's business profile to another. As stated earlier, marketing or sales operations may be the central resource for customer profiles, and marketing may have the most skilled resources for any secondary research used to fill industry-wide or publicly available information.

Key Take-Aways

Corporate Leaders: Everybody in your company needs business acumen. This is not just an HR morale-boosting pitch, but a declaration that bringing your organization along on a customer-value-focused journey requires that they have basic business literacy. Everyone in your company should understand your customers more intimately and be able to anticipate customer challenges more rapidly. As it turns out, this same business acumen gives them a more insightful view of their role within your own company. It helps them anticipate challenges for you as well.

Sales Leaders: To be trusted advisors to your customers, your salespeople need to deserve trust. There is no substitute for a salesperson who knows the customer's business as well as they do. Combining that with their expertise in your product or service becomes a real competitive advantage. Business acumen is a great investment. This chapter lays the groundwork for general business acumen.

Sales Enablement Leaders: Standing up an organizational competency in profiling prospective customers should involve your organization, probably heavily. There should be some give and take in terms of defining the appropriate sections for your business. One rule of thumb: businesses with customers in many businesses (banks and furniture companies come to mind) should push business profiling acumen close to/down to sellers, while single industry businesses (say, surgical torque drivers for orthopedic screws), can provide a generic profile, with instruction on typical individual variations to watch for.

Sales Operations: Business profiles may be a resource you need to store, maintain, and or curate. Understand what they are and how they help sellers differentiate themselves, so you can provide profiles that uncover value.

Sellers: Understanding how your customers view their own world helps you have more customer-focused conversations. The simple seven forces model enables you to gain a rapid understanding of what your customer sees every day when they go to work. **Key/Strategic Account Managers** should consider seven forces analysis as the price of entry; they should have done a thorough seven forces analysis before the first conversation with your strategic account.

Marketing Professionals: If outcome-oriented marketing is the most impactful, marketing professionals need insights into the kinds of outcomes prospective customers are looking for. Basic business acumen is a foundational capability in a value-focused marketing group.

Product/Service Professionals: When you are learning about the environment and the challenges your customers face, you'll often surprise yourself with some of the innovative (often inexpensive) ways you can deliver superior results to a customer. The seven forces model gives you and your team a "quick scan" capability.

Chapter

SIX

Financial Acumen for the "Non-Mathlete"

In the last chapter, we discussed basic business acumen. I deferred most of the math-related discussion to this chapter, which might be called "The seller's essentials to understanding financial statements" or "how non-mathletes can get as good an understanding of a business as a finance whiz."

I have a business degree from one of the country's best business schools and was in commercial finance for almost a decade. Take it from me: if you don't have high-level financial training, you can still learn a lot about a business by reading their financial reports the easy way. The hard work in this chapter was mine; to make this as easy as possible for you, dear reader.

An important note: In some businesses, like corporate finance, banking, etc. high-level financial analysis is an absolute must...for you, this chapter is too elementary anyway. I won't be helping anyone in those businesses analyze numbers faster or better. I will, though, be pointing to some of the areas that many in those industries overlook, though.

If somebody wishes to learn how to analyze financial statements, I support them wholeheartedly. You'll be a better investor in your personal life, for starters. That being said, it's important to know what financials <u>are and are not</u> good for:

Financial statements are usually used to measure the financial health of an organization. However, certain sections also provide a view of the operational health of an organization. For sellers, that's often more relevant.

Learning about a prospect's operational health is almost always a seller's real objective. We're looking for value gaps. Financial results are a symptom that a value gap might exist, but seldom provide enough detail to diagnose value gaps thoroughly.

This chapter will primarily focus on financials you can obtain from a public company, a government entity, or many non-profits. Private companies, since they don't release financials, are more challenging to analyze. Don't lose all hope, though: I'll give additional guidance on private companies as well.

Sources to Review Before Digging into Numbers

There are many sources that you should explore in addition to financial statements. These can point you toward greater – certainly different -- insights. For instance, public companies regularly give briefings to investors and stock analysts, and most will post recordings and/or copies of the slide shows from these briefings. Quarterly earnings calls can be great sources for insights: you get to hear executives answer questions from analysts who study these companies carefully…analysts who have done a lot of work diagnosing that company's health, and whose questions very quickly point to areas you should be interested in as well.

Some stock analyst reports will discuss the business prospects (Look for fundamental stock analysis; I find limited value in reports which lean too heavily on technical analysis[33], though).

> *If you have any investments, many brokerage accounts come with access to analyst reports from a number of analyst houses.*

Both public and private companies talk about themselves on their websites, in their press releases, and in industry communications. If executives (especially of privately held companies) have given talks at industry events, or have been interviewed for any publication, those are super-valuable views into the company.

You can also talk to industry experts, consultants, and ex-employees.

Does this feel like "stalking 101"? Good. Embrace it. Now let's talk about company financial reports.

---

[33] **Technical analysis** analyzes movement of a stock price/market sentiment to predict future price moves, whereas *fundamental analysis* looks at industry and company trends and analysis. Without stoking a debate over which is the superior approach to stock investors, "fundie" work is more useful for our purposes in hunting for value. If a report discusses a stock *price chart*, for instance, that's a sign that it is using technical analysis. Here's a good initial discussion for more depth: https://www.investopedia.com/ask/answers/131.asp

Once You Have the Financial Statements, Start Outside the Numbers

Before looking at any numbers, read the text that accompanies a financial statement. *Management's discussion* and *the CEO's letter to shareholders* give a great window into the numbers you are about to review…these show you what that company's management thinks about their own business. You will learn more about *how they view* their market, how they go to market, and the major risks management thinks they face (occasionally different than the risks they actually do face; *that* can be the source of some tremendous value-finding discussions!).

You need to develop an ability to read between the lines to see what isn't said as well as what is. Management's discussion and notes in financial statements were written to fulfill a legal requirement to disclose without giving competitors any more information than absolutely necessary. They do satisfy a disclosure requirement, though, so take advantage. You will see management priorities highlighted, which means you know a top management priority being communicated to the organization. If your offer can impact one of these priorities, you can offer some high-visibility value.

Financial Statements: Communicating a Company's Ability to Make Profit

I'm kind of curmudgeon about pricing and profits. I have been known to quote Charles F. Abbott:

"Business without profit is not business any more than a pickle is candy."

If you aren't going to make a profit, you should just convert to 501(c)3 non-profit status and obtain favorable tax treatment and reduced postal rates. Admit it to yourself: you're a charity.

So, what is profit? Because profit plays multiple roles in the business world, that question has a couple of answers.

Profit is one measure of business success…a pretty important one. If a company is living their purpose "providing more customer value (pricing value correctly) than it costs to deliver (which assumes capability, cost control, and having chosen the right markets/customers)," profits are the result.

Profit is what gives any company the ability to weather hardships like recessions, fund innovation, expand into new markets and ventures, and reward stakeholders.

Generally Accepted Accounting Principles (GAAP) allow several definitions of profit. Non-GAAP profit is a common term (again, without one single meaning) meant to communicate company performance in some useful way not allowed under GAAP. Amazon's Jeff Bezos understood the difference during a streak of 80 consecutive quarters of non-"profitability" (by GAAP reporting standards).

> *GAAP gives companies multiple ways to depreciate assets, value inventories, treat R&D investments, and even how/when to recognize revenue. As a result, "profit," even though it looks like a standard calculation, has many possible definitions under GAAP (in my business school, accounting students sarcastically referred to the acronym as "generating arbitrary accounting profits).*

Profit is generally a calculation using "revenues" minus "costs" (quotes added because neither of those two has a single definition), but your costs shouldn't be the basis for your prices…value should be.

Profit is the solution to *every* problem *every* CEO has *ever* had. As a result, anyone looking for customer-perceived value had better develop sufficient financial acumen to help a customer where they appreciate it most: their profitability, however they define it.

If you look at the notes above, you can see why unquestioning belief in published financials doesn't get a value hunter very far. It's more important to know what's behind the numbers you're reading than to be able to calculate precise financial ratios. Unfortunately (for the non-"mathletes," at least), you do need to know some key financial concepts.

Financial Acumen: Necessary for all Professionals… Necessary Evil for Many Sales Professionals

Every organization could up-skill their people in the area of financial acumen, but not every person needs the same level of expertise. This could vary by:

- A person's role in an organization. Everyone should understand how their job function builds – or could build – value in a customer's mind, but not everyone needs to build that case in detail.

- The company's products and/or services. The business you're in might dictate a greater or lesser degree of financial acumen – commercial lending business demands financial statement fluency as a basic job requirement, for instance.

It *does not depend on* whether your business calls on many customer types (like bankers or office equipment companies) or if you sell to a single vertical (say, oil drillers, K-12 school districts, open-pit mine operators, or hand surgeons). In single-vertical businesses, you still need the same financial skills, but it's simply easier to look at a prospect's business with more insight. Since *you should always compare a target company's numbers to peers*, single-industry sellers are simply able to compare more readily.

While I happily work with clients to develop programs tailored to their individual circumstances, I'll introduce the basics here. I'm happy to help you adjust from there.

For those who want to become more masterful in their analysis of financial statements, there are many resources and training courses widely available. If you are beginning your journey into the realm, I recommend a few resources[34] to gain basic financial statement literacy. There are great reasons to go deeper than the next few pages take you, but you can also be confident that mastering these basics will open the door to some valuable new perspectives with customers.

> *You'll do well to take Warren Buffet's advice that you learn at least as much by reading financial statement footnotes as you do by mastering the numbers.*

Cost Structure: The Financials You Want Most are the Ones That Don't Get Shared

To uncover customer value gaps, an understanding of managerial (non-financial) accounting and breakeven analysis is usually more useful than standard GAAP financial statements. Sales professionals in most industries need to know what aspects of a customer's business have the best "profit leverage": the most significant effect on profits.

When hunting for customer-perceived value, the highest "profit leverage" aspects of the customer are obviously the most productive places to search. To do this, you need to understand a prospective customer's cost structure: fixed costs, variable costs, and breakeven analysis.

The major components of cost structure are as follows. I'll show you how to find these different costs later in this chapter. First, I want to show you why they are so relevant and useful. The components of cost structure are:

---

[34] Here are a few sources which provide a great introduction to financial statements:

https://www.sec.gov/reportspubs/investor-publications/investorpubsbegfinstmtguidehtm.html

https://www.thebalance.com/formulas-calculations-and-ratios-for-the-income-statement-357575

https://www.thebalance.com/guide-to-understanding-financial-statements-357512

http://www.dummies.com/business/accounting/10-tips-reading-financial-report/

<u>Variable, or direct costs</u>: costs that directly increase as the result of producing a product or service for a customer. Raw materials, purchased components, and assembly labor costs for a manufactured product are examples. A service business like a restaurant consumes ingredients as orders are prepared. Producing more product means incurring more direct costs, and these costs readily go down when orders drop off.

> When a hotel rents a room, the direct costs incurred to provide one guest a great stay are maid service, laundry, some HVAC energy, water, a few toiletries in little bottles, a booking agent fee, and perhaps a franchise fee. This is relatively small in comparison to the nightly room rate, which means hotels are super-profitable, right? Read on…

<u>Fixed, or period costs</u>: costs which don't change – or don't change much – when a customer is served. The term period costs correctly identify that these costs "don't sleep"; they occur with regularity, every period (like monthly or yearly). In your personal life, think of the mortgage or rent you pay; it doesn't change whether the place is abandoned or filled to the brim with houseguests. It's sometimes useful to break down period costs into two types:

<u>Fixed capital costs</u>: Long-lived purchases, usually large investments. Buildings, aircraft, machines, vehicles, pipelines, etc. On financial statements, these are subjected to an accounting treatment called depreciation and/or amortization, which means that the total cost of an asset is spread across multiple accounting periods (months, quarter, year) throughout the "useful life" of that asset.

> That hotel with the low variable costs has substantial real estate costs, with a long useful life. The hotel's computer system will have a shorter useful life, and its total cost is depreciated over a smaller number of periods.

<u>Period expenses</u>: Ongoing expenses which are insensitive (at least mostly) to the activity of serving customers.

> Examples in our hotel would be property taxes, some utilities, routine repairs, and salaries in accounting, HR, front desk, security, and maintenance.

Some expenses look mixed: part fixed, part variable. That is, they can be reduced with lower company activity usage, but not to zero (many utility bills never go to zero even if you don't consume anything). There are mathematical techniques for defining the precise mix, but for the purposes of value-hunting, we can largely ignore the finer points (be assured that they are fascinating discussions within the cost accounting profession). In the vast majority of cases, your coming to a customer with even a roughly accurate idea of their cost structure will build a lot of credibility, and you can decide on whether your particular situation merits additional precision.

Costs and expenses do not appear clearly as fixed/variable in even a public company's financial statements. You need to tease them out. The reason it's worth the effort is what you learn when you have them.

Breakeven Analysis

Learning the basic cost structure (fixed and variable costs) of a prospect enables you to understand their breakeven point and where they are currently operating in relation to it. More importantly, you'll have a better idea of what kinds of changes they can make to their operations to get them (further) above breakeven.

For those who aren't familiar with the idea of breakeven analysis, here's an introduction:

Since fixed/period costs are incurred with or without any revenue-producing activity, they represent a financial hole every period (such as per month).

To work out of the hole, the company engages in revenue-producing activity. Each unit of product or service sold has a profit margin (per unit revenue minus direct costs). This per-unit margin *contributes* toward digging the company out of the fixed cost hole. Thus, it's called *contribution margin.* The quantity of units it takes to dig entirely out of the hole is called the breakeven point. The breakeven point is commonly given in dollars of revenue, but sometimes in units.

Breakeven is a function of how deep the hole is and how quickly each unit sold – the gross margin per unit – digs the company out of the hole (and thus the steepness/slope of the line).

Here it is represented as a graph. The hole, fixed costs, are shown at the left of the graph – at sales of zero. Each sale contributes some margin dollars to filling the hole until reaching the breakeven point when profits go from negative to positive.

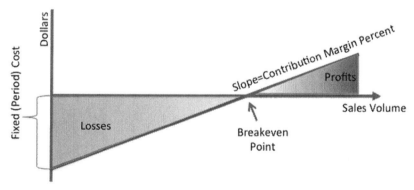

Figure 6.1 Breakeven analysis graph.

As you can see, the steeper the slope of the contribution margin line, the faster the company breaks even. Also, the smaller the fixed cost "hole," the faster the company reaches breakeven.

For the more mathematically inclined, you can calculate a breakeven point in dollars, B by dividing total fixed costs, F, by Contribution Margin (Revenue, R, minus Variable costs, V), thus:

$$B= F/(R-V)$$

Spelled out:
Breakeven = (Fixed Costs)/(contribution margin) or
Breakeven = (Fixed Costs)/(Revenues − Variable Costs)

How to Evaluate the Breakeven Point and Performance of a Customer

There are three insights to be gained from the breakeven analysis:

1. What typical looks like; that is, how a specific company compares to its peers in the same business,

2. Whether the company's breakeven has been changing recently.

3. How does your offer affect the company's breakeven, or performance against its breakeven?

Breakeven Relative to Peers

Any business will have a typical break-even point: Airlines might be similar, full-service hotels could have a typical breakeven structure (limited-service hotels as well, although a different breakeven than their full-service cousins). Breakeven analysis lets you know how that company can most effectively increase profits, and thus, where a company's priorities might lie. Competitors estimate each other's cost structures when predicting one another's strategies. Sellers should do the same for similar reasons.

If a target company lags their peers, they know it and either want to do something about it...or have made a strategic choice to be that way; figure out which and see if you can positively impact their business. If they have a superior position, ask how they got there and what that gets them.

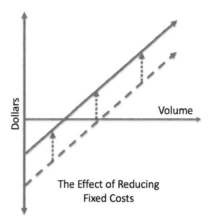

Figure 6.2 The effect on break-even of reducing fixed costs.

By flying an all-Boeing 737 fleet, Southwest Airlines has streamlined its fixed maintenance and support (aircrew training, ground equipment, ease of crew switching) costs, driving its breakeven favorably (shifting the line upward). This lower capacity aircraft drives them to a higher frequency between some city pairs. This fixed cost decision points Southwest away from longer routes, …which, in turn, places a premium on fast, convenient connections and quick turnaround capability.

To gain insight about a given prospect, you need to compare that company to its industry peers, comparing an industry-average breakeven to that of the target firm. Companies that achieve above-average margins are usually purposeful in how they do it and are likely pursuing a product leadership or customer-focus value discipline.

Next, look at a company's cost structure over time. Have fixed costs been rising? Have margins been rising or falling? Why? Has it been part of a strategic plan, by accident, or because of competitive margin compression? The senior management of a company will be paying attention to these issues. If they are experiencing erosion, it may be a point of emphasis…improving it is a priority.

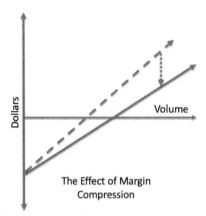

Figure 6.3 *The effect on breakeven of price/margin compression (or increased variable costs)*

A company with substantial existing fixed capital costs already on its books can't do much about them in the short-to-medium term (other than some off balance sheet financing solutions). If a company is just above break-even, they will find high value for offers that increase volume or margins. If you sell capital equipment, make sure you are well aware of how the company's variable costs, other fixed expenses, or sales might change when they utilize your solution.

Bottom line: understanding a customer's cost structure gives substantial clues to the most effective levers they have to generate more profits. Whatever you can do to impact these profit levers is a powerful proposition with high potential value.

The problem with the breakeven analysis is that variable and fixed cost reporting is not part of normal financial disclosures. You need to pull it out of the financial reports that you do have...an estimation exercise. Let's explore how to go about it.

Prospect Financial Statements

Now that we've learned the importance of cost structure analysis, we need to show you how to translate normal financial statements.

Companies release financial statements whose format is dictated by regulators and the accounting profession. These are (more or less) standardized reports that allow financial professionals to quantify the company's *financial health* on a variety of measures:

- Profitability
- Cash flow, and availability of cash

- Effective use of/allocation of capital, etc.

Again, there is value in gaining financial fluency, but I recommend simple financial analysis without bogging value hunters down in the more detailed and general-purpose courses you can find elsewhere.

Reading and Interpreting the Numbers

A cardinal rule of understanding financial statements: **everything is relative.** Just like with breakeven analysis, you need to look at company trends over time, and compared to industry averages. You can tell quite a bit if you know what "normal" looks like for individual business type, not just general industry; imagine analyzing a hotel (highly fixed asset-intensive) vs. a hotel franchisor (the company running the reservation system for the chain of franchisee hotels) vs. a hotel/casino business. Would comparing one to another – or to an average made up of a mix – tell you anything about keys to success?

Look at differences in expense patterns, such as if one peer spends more on marketing and another spends more on R&D. While there are often differences in how companies classify expenses into the categories shown on public accounting statements, you can learn a lot from any significant differences.

I always translate standard GAAP-compliant financial statements into variable costing statements[35]. Doing it precisely is hard, but I can get close rapidly and easily. Think of each line item in a public financial statement in terms of how "purely variable or fixed" that item is and translate the income statement into a cost structure analysis.

When trying to analyze private companies, I'll start with any public competitor's financial statement, and then do my own research into how the target company differs from that "norm." Often, a prospect is happy to share this kind of information willingly…if you build credibility, then ask nicely.

Variable costs: Try to identify expense lines that look variable or mostly so. For most companies' financial statements, Cost of Goods Sold on the income statement is almost purely a variable cost line. Cost of sales and Marketing Expenses are typically mixed – the variable cost percentage depends on the company and industry; for instance, if a company uses channel partners heavily (You'll find they use rep firms, distributors and the like in a management discussion section), you might expect that cost of sales is more variable than a firm who uses a direct sales force.

---

[35] If you would like to dive further into this subject, a great place to start is this article: https://bizfluent.com/how-12009134-determine-variable-costs-financial-statements.html

<u>Fixed capital costs</u> don't appear as such in financial statements. They appear as depreciation and amortization lines on the income statement (as those investments get depreciated over several years).

Fixed capital costs are where the non-financially fluent can get lost quickly. You can produce more accurate estimates if you know about how the company financed capital equipment purchases (all cash, borrowing, or lease financing), and whether they elected an accelerated depreciation method (to gain tax advantages). The additional time and expertise to get to more accurate estimates may or may not be worth it in your business.

> *Accelerated depreciation for an asset reduces taxable net income early in an asset's life, which reduces tax liability. Governments can favor certain types of assets by allowing accelerated depreciation on specific investments. Without engaging in the politics behind these decisions, a salesperson does need to be aware of when they need to look at a prospect through "corrective lenses," accounting for government-favored industries.*

If you look at fixed asset notations on the balance sheet, especially over several years, you should begin to understand any trends you spotted on the income statement regarding fixed asset-related "expenses."

Fixed period expenses are easier to identify and are usually listed straightforwardly on the income statement. Again, there are some expense categories on an income statement, which are mixtures of fixed and variable, so make your best assumptions and go from there – once again, comparing to peers and prior years for context.

As indicated earlier, the statement of cash flows reconciles the income statement with the non-cash "expenses" (mostly depreciation and amortization) to show how much cash is being generated or consumed by the business. This statement is a place to look for alarm bells; it could be a place to look for management-perceived problems, or even to identify prospects who may be in a reduced position to buy. Trends between different years are important, and any notable observations you make should be discussed by management in the management's discussion – that you already combed through, right?

Looking at all of these things, you should begin to get a high-level picture of how a target company's top executives view the company's direction and performance. You may also spot some opportunities to help. If you can connect whatever it is you sell to one of the big-picture trends you spot or are in a position to help them mitigate a significant risk (acknowledged or unacknowledged by management), your time with these documents has been invested well.

Key Take-Aways

Corporate Leaders: Everybody in your company needs business acumen to understand your customers more intimately and to anticipate customer challenges more rapidly. If you believe in empowering your people to find solutions to your business problems, it doesn't hurt to share your company's cost structure, so that they can self-analyze suggestions.

Sales Leaders: There are many courses in understanding financial statements and doing financial ratio analysis. While I don't necessarily think these are a waste of time, my extensive experience with analyzing financials leads me to believe that most of these classes are derivatives of standard accounting and finance courses. These courses are built for financial professionals in training, not business generalists like sales professionals. Rather than offering a recapitulation of an accounting course available from many providers, I suggest (depending on your business, and where your product/service produces value for a customer) that you give your sellers a shortcut: going into less financial depth, focusing on operational issues.

Sales Enablement Leaders: Business Acumen and basic financial literacy are key factors that will help your sellers differentiate themselves with your customers. You will need to determine how deeply your salespeople need to dive into mathematical financial analysis, and how much of the work is done by sellers vs. support people. I don't recommend standard courses for financial statement analysis – at least by themselves. Make sure that training and analysis focus on how to interpret management discussion, CEO's letter, investor calls, and presentations, fundamental stock analysis, and fixed/variable cost analysis more than it does financial ratio analysis.

Sales Operations Leaders: You will likely be tasked with making reports and analyses available to all types of sellers in an easy-to-digest format. Start simple, with the highest value items first, and build from there as your team sees the benefit. Don't become the barrier to adopting business acumen for your teams, which means go at their speed, explain terms, don't lapse into jargon, and provide examples.

Sellers: I want you to be able to find high-impact issues affecting your customers' businesses quickly. Understanding a customer's cost structure will help you focus on issues that will have the most value for your prospects.

Marketing Professionals: You are on the front lines of changing how your company is perceived. Understanding cost issues and key business impacts -- from your customer's perspective -- will help differentiate your company's communications, and of course, your company.

Product/Service Professionals: A clear understanding of how the business you lead fits into the customer's business, and how it can affect high priority initiatives is the key to channeling your innovation, development, and communication efforts. Whenever you are conversing with a prospective customer, this knowledge will help you reposition the conversation from technical details to business impact to your customer.

CHAPTER
SEVEN

Looking for Value Through the Customer's Eyes

Value can occur just about anywhere in your customer enterprise. Look through the business profile of a prospect to see where they may appreciate your offer's contribution... *and don't just look in all of the obvious places.* Look at some of the ways value can be generated in a list like the one below:

Additive Value	Loss Avoidance
Increase sales	Reduce Investment
Drive product differentiation	Reduce material costs
Higher close rates	Reduce downtime
Competitor gap/weakness	Reduce labor costs
Increase prices	Reduce regulatory burden
Expand market share	Reduce support/repair/warranty costs
Enter new markets	Speed up processes (onboarding, production, etc.)
Earn new customers	Relieve a bottleneck in any process
Enable new products	Reduce product liability or other risks
Reduce time	Reduce waste
Operational	Secure a key resource
Ramp-up,	Optimize Channels
Design cycle	Regulatory Compliance

*Figure 7.1 Partial list of possible **business** value creators*

Remember: any of the value above can be discovered and/or provided by you or channel partners.

By Offering Value, Your Company Starts to *Be Of Value*

Here is how the value multiplier effect works. By delivering an offer that helps your customer achieve valued outcomes, your company starts a virtuous cycle. Companies want to do business with suppliers who make them more successful. Adding value to a customer's business tends to multiply value back to yours.

As the value you bring to your customer grows, the relationship between your two companies changes.

Different Levels of Relationship Value — How the Customer Sees You

Columbia University's Noel Capon, in his authoritative work on Key Account Management and Planning[36], identified three quality levels of the customer relationship. Miller Heiman Group's CSO Insights[37] uses five: inserting two new intermediate categories in positions two and four between Capon's at levels one, three, and five. A quick Google search will find other relationship hierarchies; four levels is a common number. Level names/labels are different but synonymous. Regardless of the number of levels, higher customer relationship levels are associated with increasing customer-valued outcomes.

A bottom-level/basic customer-vendor relationship consists of meeting customer specifications/requirements, usually accepting customer terms & conditions with little modifications. Customers see little differentiation between such suppliers and are motivated to break ties via price, delivery, payment terms, and the like.

A vendor moves up the hierarchy by exceeding specs in some customer-valued way. Price ties are broken on functional differences, sometimes even supporting modest price premiums. Personal relationships, trust, and credibility start to matter at this level since service levels might be one of the "exceeding specs" factors a seller provides.

The middle level(s) have more needs satisfaction and consultative conversations, and customers regularly connect product/service to an outcome. Sellers can have access to project leads and budget owners for these projects and can position value-for-price somewhat effectively. Personal credibility and standard business perspectives are so common at this level that they are identifying characteristics.

In the upper level(s), a complex/consensus sale turns into a *mission-critical sale*. Customers see the seller's product/service as solving their business level issues, sometimes even achieving important strategic outcomes. Some sources name these upper levels after the *interconnectedness* of such relationships. The price of the seller's offer is de-emphasized due to the value of the outcome. In many

---

[36] Capon, Noel Key Account Management and Planning, Copyright 2001 The Free Press (division of Simon and Schuster) 462 pages. This is often referred to as the Bible of Key Account management. Dr. Capon reinforces this book's basic premise that customer value is the basic goal that ultimately drives shareholder value.

[37] www.csoinsights.com, or contact me to help you locate specific research and/or access to benchmarking data.

cases, the outcome delivered can be felt multiple org chart levels above the authorized purchase signature level for the product or service itself. Suppliers have numerous cross-functional trusting relationships between functional peers, and there is a genuine partnership dynamic in play.

Customers promote vendors to higher levels as they realize customer-perceived value associated with the higher relationship level. World-class organizations become adept at helping uncover – then deliver -- the kinds of customer value that justify those promotions. The reality is that the levels of relationship are dictated by customer-perceived value; they aren't relationship levels as much as they are perceived value levels.

An important point: "relationship levels" is often an idea introduced within the context of managing a company's most important/strategic accounts[38]. The power of the value multiplier is that you can proactively maximize value is for all of your customers, not just your biggest ones.

Relationship Level Isn't Locked In - The Customer Perceives It

Another thing you will hear elsewhere: Where you fit on the value hierarchy is determined by the customer. This is only partly correct. While some customers insist on keeping vendors at a more "controllable," lower level, the selling organization can –and should—work to impact the level of the customer relationship by changing the value a customer currently perceives in the relationship. *The ability to change that perceived relationship value is why you're reading this book.* While all value is customer-perceived, there is a great deal we can do to help buyers perceive greater value in our offers.

What Kind of Value Grows a Customer's Business?

The highest levels on the hierarchy are, as the definitions indicate, contributing to outcomes enhancing the customer's competitiveness *in their markets* or accomplishing strategic initiatives. Cost-cutting yields top-level value only when the customer translates those cost savings into some business-level gain.

---

[38] Capon discusses his three levels in his highly influential Key Account Management and Planning, for instance. Miller Heiman Group uses their five levels similarly in its Large Account Management Process®. On the other hand, CSO Insights moves beyond key account application of customer levels analysis. It uses a five-level scheme to describe where *any* customer places the seller relationship. CSO Insights, however, de-emphasizes the selling organization's ability to impact perceived value, *promoting themselves* to higher levels.

> *You would expect that a customer who pursues the operational effectiveness value discipline finds cost-cutting far more compelling than does a customer seeking one of the other value disciplines. For the former, cost reduction is central to their business strategy...of course, they often implement that strategy by telling vendors how unimportant and how undifferentiated their offers are.*

You've started down the path of trying to impact the customer's priorities by analyzing their financial reports. You have learned how to expand the possibilities for value contribution by using a business profile to develop hypotheses for the value you can add. In the following chapters, you will learn where to look for even more.

To guide those searches, let's look at the ways to grow a business. If you can connect your offer to any of these, it becomes more valuable to a customer.

A classic work by McKinsey & Company proposed that managers have seven strategic levers for growth. These levers consist of optimizing and/or improving various aspects of your customer's business. I've detailed the famous "seven levers for growth" as an endnote at the end of this chapter, but here they are at a high level:

1. Improve or Optimize Products and/or Services

2. Improve Marketing

3. Improve Pricing

4. Improve Customer Service

5. Improve Distribution

6. Improve Customer Relationships

7. Improve Sales Effectiveness

The levers were created for McKinsey clients to grow their own businesses, but value-focused sellers should consider going through a list of growth strategies to stimulate ideas for "high level" value.

Knowing what your most powerful value levers are likely to be, help you plan a high-gain customer engagement.

Home Run Value

Very often, sellers offer products and services that help a customer save money. Make no mistake; cost avoidance can be highly valuable and wins a lot of sales opportunities. Let's look at the most significant value prize in the B2B selling world: profitable growth, helping a customer grow their business.

> *It can be OK to shrink your company back to profitability (or reduced losses) during tough times, but the steps taken to shrink your company are not the same steps taken to grow your company.* You can't shrink your way to growth. *I can't believe some people need to be told that.*

A business leader with profit and loss responsibility is likely to pay close attention to any offer that shows reasonable odds of growing a business. Any resource that helps a company grow is well-positioned to become a trusted advisor. For that reason, you and your sellers need to be students of growth and how to achieve it. That's the purpose of this chapter.

I have spent a career growing businesses of various kinds, and while I'm certainly no authority on cost-cutting, I have a strong belief in what it takes to build a successful business: delivering customer perceived value.

When talking about the value multiplier effect and customer value, here is a basic premise:

The best way to grow your business is to be the best option your customers have to help them grow theirs.

The value multiplier is about growing a *key account's* business.

Bringing Insights into the Customer Interaction

The whole point of business profiles and analyzing a target company is to develop likely areas of value to explore, develop, and expand. At some point, though, researching information *about* the customer turns into gathering information *from* the customer. Hypothetical and proposed value – in the mind of the customer -- needs to be validated, measured, and developed.

Sales conversations to uncover value are sometimes called discovery, needs analysis, or needs probing. Great salespeople combine questions about their value hypotheses (AKA value propositions) with open-minded listening for the hints of unplanned/surprising value gaps they can creatively explore. It's worth the time investment to plan deeply value-focused customer conversations. Excelling in this kind of customer conversation requires business acumen.

In an earlier chapter, I outlined what you should look for in a sales methodology that supports value discipline. Let's take that a little further.

Remember that value conversations need to be deeper and wider than most "value selling" training courses teach. By deep, I mean a full exploration of a single value driver, including getting the customer articulate an outcome, then detail the monetary and personal impact for themselves – ideally sharing that detail with the seller. Wide means articulating all associated outcomes (and going deep with each of those). Going both wide and deep uncover full value, the reason it's called Full Value Selling™. It is worth noting that a customer's willingness to share intimate details with a seller is highly related to the trust that has been built up. When sellers look at the world through a customer's eyes, trust and credibility are easier to build.

I regularly have the conversation with proponents of various selling programs that goes along these lines: "Deep and wide value development is compatible with my sales training. In fact, a percentage of top sellers who become experts in my sales training start doing what you describe as 'deep and wide' after a few years' mastery". My question is "if 'deep and wide' is so great that masters of your methodology teach themselves to do it eventually, shouldn't there be a methodology which teaches every one of your sellers to do it from the start?". The good news is that if your training is compatible with "wide and deep" full value selling, you don't need to throw out what you're already doing.

Shameless plug. Contact me at mark@boundyconsulting.com if you'd like to learn more.

Here's some great news: it's simple for your management team to coach deep and wide value conversations. Variations on a straightforward question: "What value do they see" are a check on how detailed value conversations have been. At one company I've worked with, the corporate culture included the universal challenge question "what's the value?". If a seller couldn't answer with some deep, monetized value insights, they were directed to dig deeper with the customer before bothering a sales support resource again.

Sales methodologies directed at "the complex sale," also known as consensus selling, should be augmented with an understanding of each persona's value perceptions. Methodologies that facilitate more efficient team selling often act as a common repository for value for a given sales opportunity. The more value your team identifies with different customer roles and personas, the more powerful your selling strategy.

Proposals that tie points in the offer document directly to value drivers and outcomes don't close themselves, but they're pretty darn powerful. Combining descriptions of outcomes with the (monetary if possible) business and personal (in an appropriate format) results that prospective customers are almost always more powerful than vendor-provided ROI and cost justification models. Customer-articulated monetary outcome figures are essentially pre-validated business cases...and price justifications.

Also, when only sales conducts conversations, they aren't as three-dimensional. Value-focused companies take the opportunity to train *all of their customer-*

facing people to conduct value conversations from multiple vantage points into the customer. A more complete picture of value emerges than is possible from just one (e.g., sales department) viewpoint. Sales, marketing, service, client success, and every customer-facing role collaborate to create a 360-degree customer view. This requires two things:

- An easily mastered framework for anyone in your company to uncover, discuss, and develop value.

- A simple way for these people to combine their value findings into a communal store of value insights.

The first requires a specific kind of sales training: a simple "what is value and how to talk about it with a customer" framework. The simple framework might include more formal sales skills or methodology training for those who are major points of customer interface (sales, technical sales, subject matter experts, product specialists might be examples in your company). A variety of sales skills and methodologies could be implemented, but they should build on the common language of customer value used by all. Every seller (every person who contacts a customer at any time in their normal workflow) should have the same universal value language and should know what kinds of questions to ask and responses to look for.

In Summary

All of the tools and methods we've explored so far seek to describe the customer's *situation* in some detail. Modern customers expect that sellers know the basics of their business before walking in the door, but elite sellers – value-focused sellers – do more. They develop a deep level of understanding, then use their business savvy to build a list of probable value gaps.

Uncovering value takes not only knowledge of where to look. It also requires insightful conversations. Understanding the customer's business builds a foundation for these conversations, and a good business builds that understanding rapidly. The conversation layer of business acumen combines knowing where and how value is found and having the conversational acumen/training to execute it.

Key Take-Aways

Corporate Leaders: Making sure that everyone in your company can discuss outcomes and value with customers feeds a powerful strategic advantage. As you lead your organization along a path of continuous value improvement, giving everyone visibility into typical—and potential new – areas of value, you'll find and focus your organization on highly impactful initiatives of all kinds: product, sales, marketing, etc.

Sales Leaders: Value Focus allows your selling organization to break out of conventional selling approaches. Customer conversations focused on *their value* will help your sellers become much more effective: leading more coordinated team selling efforts, more compelling offers, and more profitable customer relationships. I'm a big proponent of sales methodology but want to make sure that you can coach for customer value discovery. The idea of value contribution is a key concept in key account management/making your most important customer relationships more defensible and profitable.

Sales Enablement Leaders: This chapter is about turning the corner from pre-engagement customer analysis to face-to-face interactions. In previous chapters, we discussed how value grows and develops in the customer's mind, and I said then that there is a lot of conversational work that goes into building that customer need foundation. This chapter describes what you need to design into your sales skills and methodology training to execute a value-focused approach to your customers. I've also emphasized how important it is to have some standard level of "value-focused-customer-discussion" training for every customer-facing role in your company, and a way to capture value insights from every role in your company.

Sales Operations Leaders: A common language of value needs to be spoken by people outside of your regular sales scope. A way to collect feedback on customer value from people outside of your regular sales silos might be in your future – perhaps curated and maintained by your function, Marketing, or jointly.

Sellers: Value-focused conversations help you direct more insightful discovery and help you formulate more compelling closing plans.

Marketing Professionals: Value conversations held by all of your customer-facing roles forces marketing to support many customer-facing organizations than is traditional. Integrate your marketing language with the organization's common value language. As different organizations develop value insights into customers, markets, and segments, you may want to become the resource for a library/repository of value insights for all to use.

Product/Service Professionals: Your job will become easier when you have access to a more complete view of customer value, and how your offer impacts your customer's business. When your entire organization uses a common value language, value insights will be more impactful and actionable.

EndNote: [1]McKinsey Group's Seven Strategic Levers to Grow a Business.

McKinsey & Company developed a framework for their clients to consider ways to grow their businesses. They called the seven areas "strategic levers" for growth, meaning that corporate leaders could manipulate one or more "levers" in their attempts pursuits. As it turns out, these levers aren't just for company internal use. As a company (or non-profit organization) selling a product or service, you can use this lever framework as a guide to see if your offer can be positioned with a prospect as moving one or more levers with your customer. If you can grow your customer's top line, you have one of the strongest value propositions available.

Here are the value levers in outline form:

1. Products and/or services. Improving or optimizing what a company sells can take a few forms:
   a. Create new products/services (including improving existing products) for existing customers. If your product improves the performance or competitiveness of your customer's product, you are in a great position.
   b. Create or develop products/services for new customers (this may require changes in distribution and marketing)
   c. New products or complementary products via acquisition.

2. Marketing: Growing the company through innovation in marketing could mean:
   a. More effective targeting of existing customers (improving success rates by doing more sophisticated demand generation work or working alongside sales with an account-based marketing strategy.
   b. More effective Internet strategy: content marketing, social selling
   c. Identifying and penetrating new markets for existing or extension products
   d. Fostering alliances with complementary products and services to create a higher value composite offering

3. Pricing. This topic is my passion.
   a. While I imagine that McKinsey took the common "big consulting shop" and "pricing consultant firm" approach of aggressive pricing to gain share, or…
   b. Risky "because we can" pricing (until the customer figures out how to do away with us) …
   c. My experience guides me to include the strategy of pricing to value, using value-centric methodologies to build customer preference through higher perceived value, and pricing to match. If you can help a customer increase the value of their products, I'm confident it's possible to grow both sales and prices simultaneously.

4. Customer Service.
   a. Value innovation in the area of customer service is a real growth lever. If you can help your customers improve customer service, it's possible that you can help them translate that value into growth.

5. Distribution. I help my clients optimize channel strategies, so this is a lever I understand well. Optimizing distribution can be using distribution to:
   a. Enter new markets
      i. Geographic
      ii. Same geog, new verticals (may require new products.
   b. Same markets, different scope
   c. Optimize channel coverage. Minimizing overlap and/or expanding reach.
   d. Offer your business as a franchise or business opportunity.
   e. License your product or franchise your business model.
   f. As an introduction to the topic, I recommend the book of a former colleague, Rich Blakeman[1] , as a resource for looking more productively at channel relationships.

6. Customer Relationships. The whole point of your journey along a path of continuous value improvement is about your customer relationships. If you can help your customers improve their customer relationships, you can have added significant value to their business.
   a. You can create new value-delivery approaches[1]
   b. You might even be able to help them create new industry structure

7. Sales Effectiveness, which is my core business. If you can help improve your customer's sales effectiveness, we may need to talk about alliances.
   a. Selling more existing products to the same customers
      i. Social selling, which is an area of potential improvement for a lot of companies
      ii. Process/methodology. I work with these. While we may be competitive, we may also have potential complementary offerings.
      iii. Sales enablement and automation. If you can help facilitate salesforce training, reinforcement, coaching, or automation This is another area of focus for many companies, which makes it an area of potential value.

Acquiring new customers in existing markets. Some of these improvements can require some channel innovation too.

Part
FOUR

Mining for Value: Practical Tools for Customer-Facing Roles

Part three of this book outlined a detailed, but quick, lay of the customer land; identifying potential value gaps and then briefly discussed confirming them with customers. We spent part three concentrating on how to uncover a more complete view into all of the outcomes a customer is looking for (not just the conventional ones all of our competitors sell to). Part three detailed the left-hand oval on the Venn Diagram below: the customer's desired outcomes or value gaps.

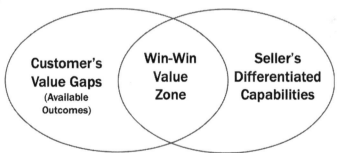

Figure P4.1 Venn diagram depicting the intersection of "what customers want" and "what the seller does really well."

In part one, though, we explained that value stems from differentiation; that is, a customer values something differentiated in our offer, which closes one of their value gaps. All commercial value for your solution lies in the overlap between the two Venn ovals.

Here in part four, we will talk about how many and which of those gaps you can help close, and what value closing them has to your customer. We will be exploring the right-hand circle in the Venn diagram above. The value network tool helps companies align their unique capabilities to potential customer value gaps. This will help everyone in your company uncover realizable value gaps and do so efficiently.

Chapter
EIGHT

Finding Value From Your Differentiation Out

It may seem strange to have a chapter devoted to "product push" in a book dedicated to the idea that all value is in the mind of your customer. The reality, for better or worse, is that you are in business to meet customer needs (at a profit), which means that you need to offer a product or service which delivers desired outcomes. A successful business manages the overlap between customer value gaps and valued offerings in two ways:

1. Expanding customer value gaps, especially in the seller's favor. This could be introducing previously unanticipated outcomes or sensitizing them to unanticipated gaps.

2. Creating or discovering differentiation that fills customer gaps. This includes both innovating new offers and uncovering new capabilities of existing offers.

> *This is similar to what marketing calls this the "unique selling proposition." In one-to-many messaging, marketing needs to choose differentiators more narrowly, so that they have universal appeal. Sales uses these, but also more individual and persona-specific differentiators.*

Value gap discovery & development practices help sellers recognize the many areas of the customer's business their solution impacts – the "customer pull" approach. We turn now to refining how we differentiate and how to talk about the differentiation we offer.

The Trap: Fist Fighting in the Phone Booth

Recall that sellers often trap themselves by working in an undersized competitive box: selling only the value customers and competitors are familiar with discussing. Selling to the conventional value propositions limits your ability to differentiate.

> *In my experience, the "undersized competitive box" is reinforced by too-narrow product training, which only teaches a narrow set of problems and solutions. Narrow feature/benefit materials lists of only the most highly predictable personas, vanilla playbooks, and more contribute to "tunnel vision."*

You probably don't need new products or services to work your way out of the phone booth. A given differentiator often produces value in multiple "landing points" throughout an organization, often outside of the department who owns the budget for buying your offer.

> For example, software that prints and mails a city's water bills is purchased by IT, the water department, finance, etc., but if it produces fewer billing errors than competitive systems, don't you think the city services call center manager, city manager, city councilpersons, and/or mayor might want to be engaged in order to express their preferences?

Many sellers work to leverage only the most conventional "landing points" in their marketing and sales strategies. As a result, these conventional selling points are easily combatted by competitors, decreasing differentiation. The problem: as other differentiation diminishes, the importance of price increases, because that's the only differentiator left.

Types of Differentiation

Companies – and sales professionals – know they must fight commoditization with differentiation. However, not all differentiation is the same (Even differentiation has differentiation!). Let's outline some of the main categories.

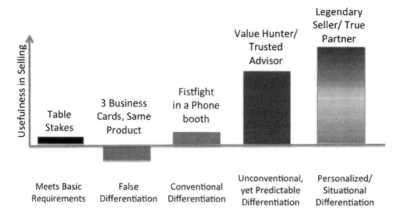

Figure 8.1 The types of business value

The graphic above represents five types of differentiation that businesses use to create customer value. The point is to understand that some types of differentiation/value are more useful in selling than others. In fact, one has negative value; it hurts your chances. Let's go through them from left to right. As you read these, give yourself a good hard look in the mirror. Which are you using well?

Confirming that your product/service meets basic requirements is of some use in selling. In many B2B buying processes, there are personas dedicated to verifying that your offer "checks the boxes." As a result, differentiators in this level are useful to stay in the game: they amount to **Table Stakes**. They are only "differentiation" insofar as they keep you from being excluded. They have a limited role in a final buying decision. This kind of information often resides in spec sheets – it should enter sales conversations and demonstrations *only when table stakes personas are present* **and** *confirming table stakes issues –preferably after offering to take such discussions into a separate conversation.* Psychologically, you shouldn't clutter other persona's minds with decision-irrelevant information (such as all the ways your offer is like all others).

False Differentiation is the second type of differentiation; the one harmful to selling. The main competitors all claim the same advantage. A customer once described this layer of value to me as follows:

"I have three different sellers' business cards on my desk, but they all sell the exact same product, under three different logos."

Brochures and websites are often inadvertent culprits; marketers want to promote the brand and don't sharply distinguish brand messaging (usually large, generalized claims, possibly about the company) from sales messaging. Regardless of the cause, the problem is that many sellers get lulled into using *False Differentiation* messages by failing to provide differentiation that matters to a customer. This impacts the buying decision negatively: false differentiation communicates a dangerous message to a prospect. At best, it's making a motivated prospect perform unnecessary work to search for true differentiation. At worst, it's "I'm proving to you that I don't have any real advantages for you to consider."

The key point to incorporate into all customer communications: information that doesn't create differentiation crowds out your uniqueness. If you sprinkle a prospect with true differentiation hidden within a geyser of "same as everyone else" messaging, you're violating the "humans find efficient ways to get on with it" principle.

False differentiation crowds out true differentiation. You are making a prospect work harder to find your value, hoping *they* find advantages you inadvertently hid in a pile of similarities. You're "playing where's Waldo" with your value. What do you expect customers to do with that? Buy?

Selling **obvious/conventional differentiation** is the middle type on the graph. This type is "easy to pitch, hard to differentiate." Conventional selling conversations are easy. The pitfall, though, is that they are the same conversations every competitor is expert at countering. With obvious differentiation, **selling has the feel of fist-fighting in a phone booth**, because *nobody can land a solid punch.* You can win sales with conventional value propositions, but seldom at satisfactory margins, because "value premiums" vs. competing offers are small and vulnerable to discounting.

There's another challenge. One of the fundamental tactics in complex/consensus selling is to find one or more buying personas (someone with a role in the buying decision) willing to help, influencing the group buying dynamic (these special personas are called champions, coaches, advocates, etc.). In the phone booth, with only minor perceived differences, few personas are motivated to risk being your champion. A problematic sale becomes even more so.

Perhaps the most damaging part of this trap is how poorly it positions a company's salespeople. When a company's sales training only covers these familiar basics, poorly prepared salespeople aren't seen as valued resources. Thus, they are seldom invited to talk with customers until relatively late, after customers have already self-diagnosed needs. This, in turn, limits 0ability to differentiate, because many opportunities to expand value gaps are closed. It's a bad cycle.

Unconventional yet predictable differentiation is the fourth type and is where radical value focus starts. Combining general business acumen with an understanding of an offer's differentiation, sellers find "out-of-the-box landing points" for value *that are common to multiple customers* (and therefore predictable). Value networks (keep reading this chapter) help sellers predict outcomes their product or service's unique attributes deliver in a customer's business. Using differentiation in the third (conventional) layer, customer insights uncover previously undisclosed value...and fresh, powerful selling approaches.

Uncovering unconventional value requires both business and customer acumen; this kind of value requires looking at your product or service through your customer's eyes. Level four differentiation is not only powerful in selling, but it also positions a seller as a **trusted advisor**, someone who can provide insight and perspective into the customer's broader business issues.

Thus, begins a cycle of credibility-building for both seller and selling organization. Differentiators often produce compelling value for the customer. Compelling value invites somebody in the buying ecosystem to become a decision lever (champion, coach, advocate, etc.). Champions help unlock value in even wider expanses of the target organization.

The key with these value drivers is that they are simultaneously unconventional (few competitors bother to work them), but still predictable. They apply to opportunity after opportunity (at least in similar customers). Thus, you can build marketing and predictive sales strategies around them.

> An example might be a device that reduces nausea in surgical patients. Conventional selling approaches might include clinicians (doctors), payors (insurance companies, in the US), purchasing, and nurses. However, reducing nausea also impacts the length of stay and sometimes complication rates – this should greatly interest unconventional personas: administrators, revenue cycle management, and risk management.

Because the value of these differentiation impacts is repeatable, sellers can be trained where to look: to uncover value by following value predictions. The second skill set required is *selling the value* of each impact[39].

Personalized, or situation-specific differentiation makes up the far-right type. These differentiators can drive either business or personal value for some persona in the buying organization.

> An example: A commercial real estate loan structured to save a business owner almost $80,000 in resolving a particular estate-planning issue. Obviously, this had nothing to do with the business, the property, the underwriting criteria of the loan. This provision was so deep in the contract terms that it wasn't even covered in the thirteen-page term sheet (offering memo). Nonetheless, it had a substantial personal impact on one (highly important) persona in the buying decision.

Individually, these differentiators are hard to build a business on, but sellers who uncover and recognize them can take advantage and use them to win opportunities. Like type four impacts, they are high-impact and high-leverage when uncovered, but uncovering them with consistency takes slightly different skills. Some sellers can repeatedly find one-off value creators, and there is a method to what they do.

In contrast to type four, where value hunters are taught "*where to look*," best practices in level five involve "*how to look*": **legendary seller** conversational skills. Every seller's job is to find value competitors don't, and sellers with a keen "nose for value" regularly find person-specific value to either win or bolster the Full Value Picture (more about Full Value later). While these value drivers are one-offs, the ability to look for them is based upon strong business and customer acumen – plus excellent interpersonal skills. A profoundly

---

[39] Because these kinds of value are repeatable/recurring, they can be trained for. Knowing where to look can be operationalized: trained, tracked, and coached.

insightful understanding of the customer is augmented by credibility and great listening (the latter often builds the former. Both require deep customer focus and empathy).

These highly individualized value drivers further cement the seller's credibility as a **true partner:** somebody with deep insight into the business as well as the personal interests of those involved in the decision dynamic. A type five value seller brings value to the client and builds strong personal trust.

The Value Network: A Tool to Uncover Unconventional Value

I've been mercilessly teasing another tool, value networks, to use in combination with business profiles and other selling tools. Value networks describe the web of value relationships in more actionable detail. They help develop the "Obvious, high-probability, and situation-specific" value layers described above. When you know a customer's business and are proficient at building/using predictive value networks, you can align your offers to a holistic set of well-developed value gaps...customer wide.

I'm repeating a table from earlier in the book, which reinforces that value can occur just about anywhere in your customer enterprise. This list is interesting but generic. It doesn't take your differentiation and market advantages into account.

Additive Value	Loss Avoidance
Increase sales	Reduce Investment
Drive product differentiation	Reduce material costs
Higher close rates	Reduce downtime
Competitor gap/weakness	Reduce labor costs
Increase prices	Reduce regulatory burden
Expand market share	Reduce support/repair/warranty costs
Enter new markets	Speed up processes (onboarding, production, etc.)
Earn new customers	Relieve a bottleneck in any process
Enable new products	Reduce product liability or other risks
Reduce time	Reduce waste
Operational	Secure a key resource
Ramp-up,	Optimize Channels
Design cycle	Regulatory Compliance

*Figure 8.2 Partial list of possible **business** value creators (figure 7.1 duplicated for reference)*

Considering each item on a checklist like the one above can direct seller time better than no search criteria at all, but we can do better. Enter the value network.

From Single-Threaded Value to Value Networks

As everyone in your company learns about how your offer (product or service) is differentiated from other options, it's essential to understand how every single differentiator impacts many parts of the customer's organization.

Any given differentiator (advantage) your product offers can have value "tentacles" that deliver improved outcomes into many parts of the organization. A visual representation, or map, of those related value impacts/outcomes, is a value network.

Value is the impact of your differentiation.

Value is built on a foundation of differentiation. Your product developers, engineers, underwriters, etc. work hard to produce differentiation. These differentiators—and their connected outcomes -- are what marketers and sellers should leverage collaboratively. Value networks are meant to maximize the return on those investments in differentiation by leveraging the value in each tentacle.

The goal of both sales and marketing is uncovering differentiators, then develop value.

A value network is a diagram mapping all points of impact/roles/personas a given differentiator has in your target company

To create a value network:

1. Pick one value driver or differentiator.

2. Write it down. When I'm introducing value networks, we write the differentiator on the top center of a poster-sized flip chart. Draw a rectangle around the value driver.

3. Now, look at your target's business. The target can be an individual company or broadened to any appropriate market segmentation. Write any results/outcomes a customer can achieve from this value driver, drawing a line from the differentiator to the result. If your differentiator impacts a significant cost or facilitates a key management initiative, diagram it.

Use the business profile as a guide that describes key activities and processes that your differentiator might be able to impact; it suggests valued outcomes.

1. Repeat for any additional outcomes.

2. Now, try to anticipate follow-on effects. Some will result directly from each differentiator/value driver; some might be "children" of other results. From each "parent" (including the differentiator), complete a sentence like [parent] "causes", "results in", or "leads to" _____[effect/impact]. Write those effects/value impacts on the paper and draw ovals around them and connect each oval to the value driver with a line.

3. Continue diagramming ideas on how that differentiator could produce value for the customer, oval those/draw lines to those as well.

4. Next, write down--next to each bubble -- who (what roles/what titles/personas) would be impacted by each outcome.

You have just produced a value network.

Who should participate in building value networks? Any seller/customer-facing contributor who might uncover value impacts should participate. This is seldom sales alone. Client services/customer success, application engineering, anyone that might understand a key function (for example if your product might impact a customer's IT group, ask a few people from your own IT group to sit in on a brainstorming session…or HR, or accounts receivable, or shipping/receiving, etc.).

Using Value Networks in Sales and Marketing.

Sales and marketing are both built around establishing and exploiting value gaps. Radically value focused companies hypothesize potential *unconventional* value gaps from predictive tools: the business profile and value networks. That is, use the profile and value networks to figure out which areas are high-probability value hunting spots, then execute a discovery strategy.

Marketing works to sensitize people to possible value gaps and help them envision outcomes. The goal is continuing and expanding the conversation with a human in sales.

At some point along the buyer's journey, a sales professional needs to contact and get initial conversations with strangers. Most sales training emphasizes *how to secure appointments*, but don't teach a strategy for *who to secure appointments with*. Most are silent when on the issue of *anticipating* which personas make good targets. Unconventional value predictions help guide salespeople to "high-value targets" (pun intended).

Sellers need a list of possible persona-specific differentiators they can use to secure appointments with every contact who might have value – even unconventional -- for a product or service.

A selling organization must predict and explore all the impacts of each differentiator. This prediction should include who in a target company might be impacted and how. For sellers, this analysis makes up a target list of contacts within a prospect.

Similarly, a seller develops a possible target list of value points.

Value gaps are uncovered and developed via face-to-face conversations. Each selling company has its own set of differentiators, and you and your company need to figure out which ones are which type (although I'm happy to help you work through it).

I won't cover "obvious/conventional" value very heavily in this book. Your most average sales and marketing people know their way around these value propositions, and just about every current sales process emphasizes them. It's more profitable to focus on types four and five. To do this, make sure that your people have business profiles, and selling tools (briefings/training/question guides) detailing value in the less obvious layers, and give them the business and customer acumen to help them find the one-offs.

A Value Network Example for a Product

Here's an example of a value network for a commercial flooring company whose carpet has a durability advantage. This value network is a general-purpose one that the company will be using for most customer opportunities:

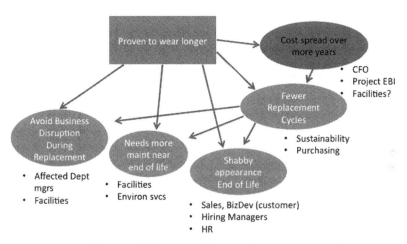

Figure 8.3 Value network for a product: carpet wear-resistance

The obvious value proposition is the darker gray oval above. The company's sellers are very used to selling at a higher price that compensates for the <u>extra years of floor life</u>. This is the fistfight in a phone booth -- that every one of their competitors can adjust for. It uses a straightforward arithmetic calculation: dollars per year (purchase price divided by service life). Thus, if my carpet lasts 20% longer, a customer should buy mine at a price premium of 19.9% or less[40].

---

[40] At a 20% price premium, dollars per year of the two options are equal, and the decision can go either way. In chapter nine, we'll describe this as "the indifference price" in more detail.

When I price at a 15% premium (to share some value with the customer), all my competitor needs to do is drop their price by 6%. I wear 20% longer but am now 21% more expensive; I lose on simple arithmetic.

Not only is conventional value easy to sell, but it's also easy for your competitor to counter.

Let's look deeper into other "landing spots" for our differentiator. Longer product life drives other possible outcomes/value impacts (reminder: before the seller validates any of them, they're *proposed* impacts):

- There are fewer replacement cycles. This means that purchasing's workload is diminished, and also that a large waste disposal problem is less frequent, which affects a sustainability officer's charter.

- While "our" carpet's appearance is sustained all the way through end-of-life, competitors' carpet *appears shabby* just before replacement. Will this be a negative value impact to anyone having important guests into the facility, and possibly to HR (concerned about company morale? It's certainly a worthwhile value hypothesis).

- "Our" soil-shedding performance lasts through end-of-life. Our carpet may need to be *cleaned less often*. Those burdened with more frequent cleaning, say, environmental services (janitorial services), could be impacted.

- Finally, and as a major value impact, flooring replacement is quite a process. There is usually around a two-day *business disruption* as furniture is moved out, flooring is removed, and then replaced (along with all the complaints about misplaced/broken items or misconnected equipment). Both installers and those departments occupying the affected spaces are all impacted. Depending on the area, this may not be over a weekend (even if it is, facilities won't be excited about the overtime and loss of personal time).

"Longer wear" lands value in many departments around the target company. The value network captures the "value tentacles," and who the value might resonate with. Importantly, the value network gives sellers an insightful discussion topic with each prospect.

All of these value proposals are just that: *proposals* that aren't *value* until they exist in the customer's mind. The value network is a pursuit guide. Using these new value propositions/potential value impacts, a seller can develop a strategy to engage strategically with all players identified. Using these value hypotheses in the value network, sellers have a strong, customer-focused justification for asking for time with these players.

Value hypotheses can then be explored, validated, and ultimately quantified.

Often, unconventional value areas contain unconventional advocates which enhance the selling strategy. I've called adding new value-realizing personas "packing the court" in your favor.

This is radical value selling: the budget for the carpeting remains with the facilities group, but the value delivered elsewhere can motivate people to express their preferences to those with budgetary ownership. This cross-functional value story is also a strong justification to involve an executive whose authority spans all affected silos.

Remember, not all value is positive. Less frequent replacement intervals don't work to the advantage of the flooring contractors and dealers, for instance. Also, a competitor may have shorter lead times, which alleviates a planning burden on certain personas. Sellers need to uncover and be responsive to value disadvantages as well. The entire company needs to be aware of advantages and disadvantages to enrich the response to any competitive value.

Most important (to someone who has managed a P&L, anyway), the price premium that this seller can achieve becomes much larger than the conventional "dollars per year" price calculation in the first yellow oval. Each value driver validated by the seller increases not only preference for "our" product but increases the defensible/achievable price premium.

This value network reflects only one product differentiator for this company's product: longer service life. In addition to longer service life, the company's salespeople should be able to create value networks for others: moisture resistance, modular replacement, resistance to specific chemicals (cleaning agents used in healthcare facilities), and more. A sales opportunity might combine a number of these differentiators, and the opportunity strategy (and ultimately any pricing strategy) should take advantage of all value nodes on all networks: I call exploring an exhaustive approach to value development **Full Value Selling™**, a key part of radical value focus.

To leverage each differentiator, salespeople should become familiar with customer costs for services related to the product, such as average costs of carpet cleaning, specialty stain removal, water remediation, and so on. Not only does this knowledge show the salesperson has "done his homework," but it provides strong arguments for cost savings in upkeep. A salesperson's estimates of these costs won't count as much as the customer's estimates; we'll discuss that in-depth later.

Value Networks for Intangibles and Services

Next, let's consider this example of an intangible: The customer is a software company's marketing organization (at least, they are the ones whose budget will pay for the service) tasked with hiring an outsourced sales organization to convert their traditional packaged/boxed software installed base to subscription model customers, also known as "Software as a Service" (SaaS). "Our" company is competing for the business by promising documented, predictable sales results. All competitors will deliver results, but "our" difference is 5% better results, documented more convincingly than a competitor's.

What price premium do you think that's worth? Answer this to yourself, then read on.

A conventional approach to the budget-owner in Marketing will be based on a cost of sales (CoS) calculation: the *predicted* incremental conversions divided by the cost of the service provider's offer.

To boost our cost of sales proposition, we could sell lower risk. We could estimate the risk difference between our service and the top competitor.

I emphasize *predicted* because the customer decides what math they will use to compare competing offers. A seller can boost their calculated CoS by increasing marketing's faith in it -- providing references and other evidence. Thus, any proof points significantly impact the forecast...and the arithmetic associated with our value premium.

> Note: I advise sellers to use customer forecasts. This avoids a lot of (truly) wasted effort. Sellers can appeal or "talk up" a customer's forecast, provide better proof points and references, bring in other experts...but ultimately, because value is in the customer's mind, the customer's forecast is the expected outcome. Because the decision will be based on the customer's forecast, theirs is the only forecast that matters. The seller's forecasts only relevant when the buyer adopts them.

The math for this value proposition looks much like the conventional price premium calculation for carpeting, doesn't it?

This approach and its math under-sells full value and places the seller at risk of winning the business with unnecessary discounting.

Figure 8.4 Value network for a service: Outsourced Inside Sales

The full value network looks more like this:

- Marketing's search for this service is all about accelerating the customer shift from software purchases to subscription-based. This differentiator falls into the conventional/obvious value layer associated with the "fistfight in a phone booth," aka Marketing's KPI.

- Higher annual revenues. While marketing *desires* higher revenues (as a basis for justifying their roles and perhaps bigger budgets), the CEO and the CFO *need* higher revenues; they are far more invested and, therefore, more motivated to achieve revenue growth. C-level executives would typically transmit a "shift revenue" KPI to marketing. Marketing takes that C-level instruction seriously, but seldom internalizes the full monetary significance to the CEO.

- Recurring revenue, especially subscription SaaS revenue, is valued by investors/stock analysts...literally. Recurring revenue streams carry a higher stock P/E ratio than conventional software revenue. This value is top-of-mind to the CEO, CFO and possibly Investor relations, but may not even be on the radar screen in Marketing.

- Lower (zero?) cost of sales for software upgrades, since SaaS places all users on the current version. The Chief revenue officer, CEO, & CFO are all over this. Relieving any product mix/sales time allocation challenges in this particular case would resonate with these leaders but would probably escape marketing's attention.

- Lower shipment and fulfillments costs drive down the cost of goods sold… elimination of CDs, packaging costs, shipping, etc. This might be a cost savings for a shipping/logistics function, as well as an impact appreciated by the company's chief sustainability officer.

- Fewer versions of software in the customer base lowers tech support costs: it's much easier to balance which customer support agents are trained on which versions on which shifts. It also reduces call resolution time by eliminating troubleshooting time around discovering software version.

For simplicity's sake let's look at this value driver in isolation/as if it's the only one for this sale.

In this network, *the Conversion KPI is still the differentiator, but the monetary value of each percentage point of uplift is many times higher* than in the simple CoS calculation marketing started out with.

In bigger companies, KPIs like conversion rate are desired for the sake of bonusing and the like. It's less frequent (but it does happen) that KPIs are as valuable to marketers as they are to the company's executives. Departments execute without a deep understanding of the why.

> *The more a company's culture represents "for-process" described in chapter one, the less likely they are even to be interested in understanding the why.*

As a result, the true value of the KPI to the company is usually under-estimated by the KPI-holder...and because it's a crowded competitor pool with hard-to-judge differentiation, the seller could be fist fighting in a phone booth. The value network details the "why" behind management's giving Marketing its KPI in the first place. Until the seller can leverage full value, they will only be able to win at a small-to-zero price premium. However, walking a customer through the value *network and validating it with many company departments/personas,* **even a small-sounding performance difference becomes decisive.**

> *Zero price premium is what happens when a customer believes you have an advantage but hasn't been influenced into doing the arithmetic. Your differentiator is simply a tiebreaker...and you never got repaid for the costs it took to develop your advantage.*

In this network, the high-value outcomes that underpin the KPI are probably outside Marketing's full awareness, and there is an opportunity to increase the importance of meeting or beating the conversion goal. Our seller should consider how to highlight all value dynamics shown in the value network. For instance, Marketing won't be able to estimate the cost/labor savings in the customer support call center, and adding a motivated ally to the buying ecosystem might be useful (bedside manner and respect for turf and not appearing to circumvent counts for a lot here).

The salesperson can prioritize her or his "value mining" project: how deeply he digs into all of the value hypotheses mapped out on the value network. He probably doesn't need to do it alone, however; there may be team discovery opportunities—that is, conducted by marketing and sellers without sales job titles.

Value Networks for Non-Profits and Your Own Internal Change-Management Initiatives

For a non-profit organization, I've developed a combined set of four interconnected value networks. These are for a set of evidence-based medical guidelines that accelerate and improve after-surgical recovery. This set of value networks is one that the non-profit is using to influence hospitals to adopt their ERAS® (enhanced recovery after surgery) guidelines. ERAS is not merely "pushing patients out the door to recover at home," but actually accelerating recovery.

In every country other than the USA, these guidelines are proven no-brainers, and adoption has been extensive over the past 15-20 years. The conventional calculation is "annual cost savings" (often tens of millions) divided by "cost to implement" (usually less than a hundred thousand). In the USA, however, "lower-cost" also means "lower revenue." The calculation becomes much more complex, which has slowed acceptance of these guidelines; fewer than 10% of US hospitals are estimated to have adopted the guidelines.

> *I don't want to turn this into an indictment of the US healthcare system, but there is a fascinating dynamic at work that a behavioral economist would find fascinating. Adoption of ERAS in the USA is complicated by how America's system separates who benefits, who buys, who pays, and who bears the cost of implementing a change. For an ERAS implementation, this disaggregation makes for a complicated set of incentives. Beneficiaries (patients) have no say in implementing ERAS. Doctors and allied medical staff bear the behavioral cost of change, but there is perceived legal risk in departing from "current standard of care," even to "provably better." Finally, ERAS reduces postoperative opioid use. Patients benefit from this, but so does society: productivity, law enforcement, societal burdens are reduced substantially. Who pays? An insurance company. It's all a crazy, fascinating mess.*

As it turns out, developing a set of value networks for ERAS uncovers significant value in unconventional places. Interestingly, while America offers the disincentive of "lower revenue," it provides higher incentives in the area of risk management/legal exposure.

The value networking exercise yielded a set of four interlinked Value Networks, as shown below.

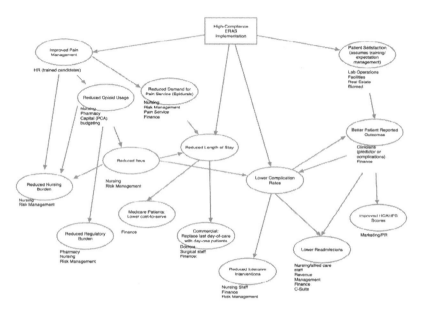

Figure 8.5 Value network for a non-profit organization: Enhanced Recovery After Surgery (ERAS) guidelines

Results of an ERAS® Implementation

ERAS incorporates several straightforward changes in a "surgical care pathway" (the entire arc of care pre- during, and post-surgery), which have a strong combined effect on patient outcomes. It's truly a combination effect: The more of these small changes a hospital makes, the stronger the effect, but none of the changes drive the effect alone. Thus, there are financial/patient welfare motivations to adopt fully, even if a given hospital's culture dictates a stepwise approach.

The four value networks contain a lot of downstream nodes, but represent the four major primary value dynamics in play:

Value Network One: Improved Pain Management

ERAS guidelines require exceptional collaboration between surgical and anesthesia specialties. Long-acting nerve blocks (epidurals are the most complex and difficult, but the most familiar) not only give patients better post-operative pain relief, they give hospitals fewer pain calls and tending fewer PCAs (Patient-controlled analgesia units, the boxes that let a patient press a button for more [usually] opiates, subject to dosage/rate limits set by a doctor or nurse). PCAs tend to push inexpensive opioid drugs, but the management costs of purchasing, tracking, maintaining and monitoring PCAs, as well as the costs of monitoring, maintaining, and recordkeeping of the patient using the PCA represents a substantial invisible cost to a hospital, significantly eroding the idea that "opioids are cheap pain relief."

Some hospitals which have implemented ERAS believe that the reduced workload probably won't translate to lower staffing levels but definitely *reduced error rates* by nursing and allied health staff. This is not error rates directly in the administration of the PCA but from a more generalized workload/distraction level.

> *I've seen figures that claim that medical errors are the third leading cause of hospital death. Administrators are always on the lookout for ways to reduce caregiver distractions.*

Another direct result of the ERAS pain management guidelines is *drastically reduced opioid* use. That is, ERAS patients don't require as many opioid drugs to manage post-op pain:

Opioids have a few disadvantages for pain management:

- Opioids are notably *ineffective on skeletal pain* (such as after hip surgery). Patients of certain specialties have a poor choice between unacceptable pain or risky levels of narcotics. This costs hospitals too. *Nursing burden* increases and *liability risk* for excessive opioid exposure (increased risk of addiction, exposure to regulatory scrutiny, etc.) is an increasing concern.

- Opioids also notably shut down peristalsis in the digestive tract. There is an increased nursing burden from increased patient discomfort, increased need for bathroom attendance, and increased length of stay.

> *Medical professionals call this slowdown ileus. TV commercials from pharma companies call this "opioid-induced constipation" ...and try to sell you a drug for it. I ignored this perverse situation in this value network.*
>
> *Surgical patients are often not allowed to be discharged unless they've had a bowel movement. No peristalsis means no discharge. Pun intended.*

- Reduced opioids carry their own direct rewards to hospitals:
  - Opioids are increasingly subject to *increased regulatory, administration, and access control burdens.* These carry a

rapidly growing set of costs, often dwarfing opioids' low acquisition price. As litigation around (claims of unnecessarily exposing patients to excessive) opioids rises, risk *management costs* (legal costs, loss reserves, settlements, avoidable PR harm) are rising substantially. ERAS implementation helps mitigate these risk management costs significantly.

o Some hospitals that are reducing opioid usage are building public awareness and advertising campaigns around this fact, trying to turn progress into public reputation and *differentiating themselves in competitive* markets.

> *As noted previously, society benefits greatly from reducing patient exposure to opioids in the hospital. Post-op opioid use is a major on-ramp to opioid addiction. Society doesn't (directly) pay for a patient's surgical stay, though.*

Value Network Two: Reduced Length of Stay

Patients who undergo ERAS-compliant care regimens go home sooner, with fewer complications, and at a significantly lower cost.

The straight cost-savings are an easy calculation for Medicare and Medicaid patients; payment for a given case is fixed, and reducing cost-to-treat has an evident profit impact.

For conventional patients, on the other hand, any hospital that is *bed-constrained* turns away patients it might otherwise wish to serve. Surgical patients tend to concentrate revenue and costs early in each surgical stay. In other words, the last day of hospitalization is the lowest cost/lowest revenue day in most surgical patients' care journey. Hospitals who can consistently replace those low-revenue last-day patients with high-revenue first-day patients increase revenue per bed per day".

Value Network Three: Lower Complication Rates

Complication rates decline as ERAS compliance increases.

The financial impact of lower readmission is in flux in the USA. Payer compensation for readmissions is currently being phased in (that is, the payer/insurer reduces or even eliminates reimbursement to a hospital who needs to readmit a patient for a surgical complication). This turns readmissions upside down: from a revenue opportunity (albeit with an elevated risk management profile) to a pure cost avoidance factor. As hospitals are increasingly compelled to absorb costs associated with readmissions, ERAS compliance becomes an instant value slam-dunk.

Complication-driven readmissions represent a legal/complaint exposure risk, which has a cost. Readmitted patients are more likely to file formal complaints, seek billing adjustments, and file lawsuits. These patients are also above average in the intensity of care. The risk of errors by nurses, doctors, residents, administrators, and scheduling is higher, and those errors tend to be more costly (if for no other reason than because they are more likely to be errors accompanied by patient dissatisfaction)

Value Network 4: Patient Satisfaction

Facilities implementing ERAS have had mixed patient satisfaction results. The primary determinant is whether there was good patient expectation setting around:

- How long they'll be in the hospital,

- How soon they will be made to get out of bed and walk,

- Missing out on an anticipated "opioid haze," even though they experience less pain.

- Generally different patient experience (vs. a friend who had the same operation elsewhere),

Patients may feel like they are being pushed out of the hospital before they're ready. Even if patients feel better sooner, some feel like they missed out on the full "legal drug use" experience and are actually disappointed. One of the costs of ERAS is around robust patient education from the outset. Only then can the benefits be realized.

Patient satisfaction, as measured by HCAHPS Scores, turns into a monetary benefit to the hospital through public release/reporting/advertising of patient satisfaction, mortality, and complication rates.

Patient-reported outcomes (PROs) are measurements of patient status (pain scores, happiness, feelings of wellbeing, and the like). They are measured as a baseline before/at the time of admission and then during the stay. These have several uses:

- They are used to measure the progress of recovery. Comparing to the baseline PRO, a caregiver can define "recovery" more objectively.

- They also serve as an early indicator of trouble, which enables rapid rescue: faster intervention. This results in a shorter length of stay (note the bidirectional relationship between PROs and length of stay. They reinforce one another).

Using these value networks, the nonprofit organization been able to show how its guidelines generate significant value to hospitals. If it had been only a question of patient value, it would be a no-brainer. The economic reality is that it's not, and they needed a tool like this to help them have more insightful conversations.

Using Value Networks in Concert

These four relatively simple value networks combine to build a compelling case for a hospital to invest in a (pretty substantial, it turns out) organizational change management program. It's difficult to convince medical professionals that "the way we've done things for decades" should give way to a more modern evidence-based approach. It gets even more complicated when the change requires coordination among many specialties (the healthcare version of "silos"). The costs of getting hospital staff in support of an ERAS initiative and trained are the primary costs of adoption.

The personas targeted by these networks have high overlap. For instance, we now have many value hypotheses to discuss with a hospital administrator (also a surgeon, CFO, CMO, etc.) The combination of many outcomes makes for a compelling case for change. Preparing for each of these conversations via constructing well-crafted value networks helps sellers (in this case, those sellers are often doctors or nurses volunteering their time to influence others) explore all outcomes, and all value – in the language of a different medical specialty. It also builds the foundation for gaining support organization-wide, the critical step in any change management initiative.

Use of a Value Network as a Change Management Tool

Administrators use this value network to formulate internal business cases for ERAS adoption in their hospitals. Without this value network, doctors wishing to adopt ERAS have regularly run into internal resistance from administrators, nursing and other staffers, etc.

At its heart, the value network is a change management tool. A sale is merely a customer's decision to change…to adopt a seller's offer. Business justification/business case conversations within the buying organization are mere money-measured calculations of impact – the value– of adoption. The process of envisioning outcomes is central to the process of gaining group buy-in. If you are a business leader, using a value network as a tool to get organization-wide buy-in to *any change management initiative* helps your entire organization see all of the value tentacles, not just their own personal "cost of behavior change."

Team Value Selling Around the Value Network

Here's a key practice: Look at the value network as a target list for a radically different team selling effort. It may be easier for some of your colleagues in client success/customer service, application engineering, deal execution/delivery/implementation to discuss certain value drivers with peers and customer contacts they interact with regularly. You might also include sellers in different geographic areas who have local contacts involved in a given opportunity.

Team selling illustrates how value focus is a company-wide discipline. It's also an easy (OK, maybe just straightforward) way to operationalize the principle of radical value focus; capturing value networks and sharing them with your product innovators closes a key information loop that turns the broad mandate of "be more customer-centric" into a clear path toward being a value-driven enterprise.

If you go to market through channel partners, remember that they are every bit as important to the team selling/organizational value focus as any other member of your organization, often with a perspective that your people can't replicate.

How Does Crafting Value Networks Enrich Sales?

First, it *adds precision and rigor to opportunity pursuits.* A value network starts as a system of value hypotheses. None of the bubbles on the value network is worth anything until a customer has validated it. The network is a map to guide the sales discovery process. Every hypothesis should find its way into a discovery meeting plan. Every validated hypothesis should enlighten an opportunity pursuit.

As part of that honesty, value networks can alert us to the reality that competitors can have value that we don't; differentiators that diminish (or even negate) our value for a given pursuit. Sales methodology provides detailed mechanics for this as the decision ecosystem gets more complex. Value analysis, though, helps sellers uncover and deal with competitive threats more efficiently.

Second, it *helps us be strategic and more creative.* Value hypotheses help uncover new potential motivated allies (personas if you're a marketer, Buying Influences in some sales methodologies) in the customer buying ecosystem. In the example value networks above, there are numbers of impacted parties who can inject extra momentum into a sale.

Note that *not all personas involved a sale are called out in a value* network:

- Process-buyers (somebody within the customer company whose role is to facilitate or guide the buying decision) may not always have a stake in the decision. These could be a purchasing person or a project leader designated by an executive from outside of the buying ecosystem.

- Subject-focused buyers. (people enlisted on a narrow subject matter, legal Ts & Cs, purchasing details, and standards compliance for instance) confirm "table stakes value," described earlier in this chapter. While they focus on making sure that specific functionality, features, or attributes of your offer meet requirements, they often aren't looking for differentiation or unique value. Thus, the value network may not hit their role.

Third, value networks also *inform team collaboration* within the selling company. This is not just a "many hands make light work" issue. Different sellers have credibility and access to different personas and can bring incredible depth to an opportunity pursuit. Doing so also drives a lot of alignment around the true north of customer value throughout many parts of your organization.

Fourth, value networks *help us be thorough*, pursuing value in radical depth. Any given sale usually has multiple differentiators in play. That, in turn, means multiple value networks. Many times, these networks overlap, providing multiple value propositions to a given party/persona in the prospect organization. The search for customer value becomes more comprehensive, more broad-reaching, and yet more tightly focused.

Fifth, value networks *tend to be modular and reusable* across multiple opportunities. If your product has higher reliability, the associated value network can be applied directly across multiple customers in the same industry (say, oil & gas), but should have strong applicability in related industries (chemical processing), and be a great start in many others (PharmBio processing, for example).

Libraries of successful value discoveries are powerful best practices sharing tools, systematizing past success.

- Sharing impactful value networks with sales colleagues can help replicate sales successes and provides a common language to replicate the behaviors of top performers. They enable world-class seller onboarding, too.

- Mapping value networks with marketers informs more impactful thought leadership, content marketing, account-based marketing, decision aids, etc.

- Customer service agents informed by value networks can provide a richer customer experience by connecting interactions with likely value drivers.

- Value networks are a great shorthand to guide product extensions and innovations

- Anyone accessing the library can use it to stimulate creative thinking in all kinds of ways.

Sixth, Value networks *improve product training*. They turn feature/benefit product training into high-leverage, customer-centric "high impact selling" sessions. A best practice in product training includes value networks to help sellers understand how products benefit customers.

Sales benefits directly and dramatically. Value networks inform:

- Who to talk to/who to look for in an opportunity pursuit

  - To have a solid basis for reaching deeper and higher within an organization when pursuing an opportunity.

  - How to approach follow-on and up-selling opportunities.

- What to talk about.

- How to compose compelling reasons to meet, helping to secure appointments more successfully.

- Highly impactful discovery that prospects appreciate more, and which builds seller credibility.

- A framework to investigate value, validate hypotheses, and monetize the value impact (which we discuss in detail in chapter 12).

Value networks can be combined with the business profile to make a thorough set of well-targeted prospecting/entry points. Let's look back at the flooring company we built our first value network for earlier in this chapter.

> The value network for "wear-resistant flooring" might be positioned one way for a customer pursuing an *operational effectiveness*[41] value discipline. An organization might lead with durability to the network of facilities personas in that value network.

> The same sellers of the same carpet might prospect differently into a software development company using pursuing customer-focused value discipline. If we analyze one of their key resources as brilliant software engineers, making recruiting a key success factor for that business, the aesthetic and low-carbon footprint parts of any value networks may be a more productive lead-in.

---

[41] Recall Treacy and Wiersema's three disciplines, Operational Excellence, Customer Focus, and Product Leadership. This is the first element of the Business profile from Chapter 5.

Pulling it all Together

In conclusion, and as a preview of a coming chapter:

> *Full value (discussed more later) is all of the impacts of all of the differentiators, measured monetarily.*

In this chapter, we've transitioned from studying the customer's situation from a distance to hypothesizing value for an individual opportunity. We've developed the idea of value networks to create a strategy to engage a prospective customer more widely and deeply.

Value networks start as educated guesses. Sometimes, they are informed by a lot of relevant experience with similar companies – or even prior pursuits at the same company. When they have been validated, they are valuable tools to inform processes throughout your company.

How Do Value Networks Enrich the Customer Experience?

I recently had a thought-provoking discussion with a colleague who told me that value is the same thing as customer experience (CX, as the cool kids know it). Thus, I should replace "value" with "CX," if for no other reason, to ride a currently trending topic/wave. CX is the experience a customer has with an organization and its product(s) or service(s), which can be measured throughout the entire relationship, or at a specific stage in the customer journey.

Even though there is indeed a lot of overlap, they are different. Value is what makes the customer experience so, well, valuable. Not every element of the customer experience delivers the same value. We design a better customer experience because we have deep value insights.

Value is the kernel inside of CX that makes CX optimization such a worthwhile pursuit. Semantics aside, value networks inform the creation of a better, more comprehensive customer experience. They help us highlight all of the personas within a customer whose experience we should incorporate into CX.

CX thinking reinforces the fact that all sellers (any role who touches the customer) are part of how a customer experiences your company, and anyone can turn into a value strength or weak link.

I appreciated the discussion with my colleague so much that I wanted to thank her here (OK, anonymously). CX thinking and value focus both promote a more holistic view, and de-siloing all of the seller organizations. Value focus focuses on proactively *gathering new value insights* while trying to delight, bringing those insights back to the organization as the foundation of even greater value-focused innovation, marketing, etc.

Elite Level Value Networks: Capability Platforms

Up to this point, we've built value networks around a feature of an existing product, service, or intangible. I hope I was able to describe the concepts -- then provide enough examples – for you to begin telling yourself a story of about how valuable these tools can be for you.

Some companies, especially those who build custom and semi-custom products & services – although not necessarily – build value networks not on product features but on capabilities.

> When I was at GE Capital, one of my biggest customers was a large structural steel contractor (providing I-beams, but mostly massive amounts of concrete rebar, aka reinforcement bar – used in reinforced-concrete construction of roads, bridges, and buildings. I sold them money: financing for buildings and equipment. The customer's most significant business risk, though, was raw material (steel) prices. They had won contracts at a fixed price but were paying spot/market prices for steel. GE's strategic accounts team connected them to GE's commodity and purchasing team to learn all there is to know about hedging and locking in future pricing – a capability that could have saved the contractor from bankruptcy if steel prices moved unfavorably.

> It took some out-of-the-box thinking – and customer insight -- to connect an organizationally-distant GE capability to this customer's most significant value gap, but you can imagine the effect on the relationship. We offered a differentiating capability that no other lender could match and leveraged it into value that reached the CEO.

Some companies self-define their capabilities into platforms. These are distinctive capabilities on which differentiation is built. Understanding what competencies in your organization drive sustainable differentiation is a strategic tool. It may take an outside set of eyes to help you look at your business differently. Once you do, value networks can help understand the full power of the differentiation you've built.

Key Take-Aways

- **Corporate Leaders:** Your company sells products or services that they work hard to differentiate. That differentiation needs to be well understood and fully leveraged if you are going to be able to charge sufficient pricing to continue and extend your differentiation strategy. Value networks are a great tool to help your entire organization understand your differentiation so you can cover the costs of producing it.

Value networks are for internal use too. Over half of all change-management initiatives fail[42]. A key failure mode is explaining the "Why" of the change. When implementing any internal change, using the value network to show the inter-related benefits highlights not only the cumulative benefit of the initiative to your enterprise, it also underscores the complex web of "who all is depending on each of you to do your part."

- **Sales Leaders:** Every one of your sellers, from those in onboarding to your seasoned producers, can find something in value layers and value networks to help them become more effective and successful. Building a language of value in your team is easier when you have a simple tool like value networks to communicate differentiators and the sales strategy implications of them.

- **Sales Enablement Leaders:** The reasons to produce, maintain, and enable your sales teams with quality value networks are many (the previous section, "How Does Crafting Value Networks Enrich Sales?" gives a great review. Bottom line, using them well will help sellers execute complex full-value selling efficiently and effectively. Value networks form a shorthand for how the best sellers in the world think of opportunities and approach their craft. They can become a critical success factor bringing every seller in your organization to a higher level.

- **Sales Operations Leaders:** I hope I've made the case for whether to adopt a discipline around using value networks. Execution will probably fall on you. The good news is that it is relatively simple to create and maintain a set of these powerful tools around your company's differentiators. Sellers often enjoy developing and adding to value networks for one another – it's easy to make value network sessions fun when the payoff is so apparent.

- **Sellers:** You probably know the dangers of "feature dump" or "show up and throw up" but haven't had a quick way of translating your differentiators into selling advantages. Value networks show the business implications and "who cares" of those business outcomes in an easy-to-digest format. Understanding the layers of value will help you understand the importance of differentiation, and which

---

[42] There are stacks of studies, some of which show greater than 50% failure rates for change management initiatives. Some show failure rates in the 40s, but define "failure" narrowly. Without arguing the exact number and definitions of success, we can all agree that getting your organization to change is a risky proposition. In my practice, for instance, the risk is all in change management, not whether the tools actually work.

differentiation types have the most significant impact on your customers.

- **Marketing Professionals:** Value networks are a goldmine for outcome-based communications. They are also a great way to communicate about products and sales strategies internally. Besides, they may also give some insight into new use cases, applications, or even product innovation. The discussion on layers of value should also serve as a set of guidelines for your content producers: being rigorous about genuine differentiation vs. false differentiation will sharpen your communications and give them a much higher impact. Finally, value networks can give you better insights into the logical and emotional buying motivations, which will improve your marketing materials.

- **Product/Service Professionals:** Value networks give product and service managers great insight into the set of customer outcomes you can and do impact. They are also a great way to communicate about products in the form of high-impact product training. In addition, they may also give some insight into new use cases, applications, or even product innovation.

Chapter

NINE

Profitability Happens at the Top Line

Business leaders have many different challenges and problems, but they all shrink in the presence of profits. I've heard that *profits solve every management problem*. That may not strictly be true, but it often feels like it. Profitability is such a powerful curative that it can mask a lot of dangerous shortcomings…but that's a topic for another book.

Here's the thing: the purpose of every company is to provide more customer value than it cost them to produce. Profit is thus the difference between value provided (if you price it properly, the topic of this chapter), and every other line on your company's income statement.

When everyone in the company is effectively and efficiently focused on customer value, lots of good things happen:

- Products become more strongly differentiated and strongly preferred. We've overviewed this already. Using customer value insights to close a product/service innovation loop has always been valuable, and while I like the idea of "the voice of the customer," it's a pale shadow of using "the mind of the customer" as a guide for innovation and differentiation.

- Content/marketing services that deepen customer perception of outcomes accelerate customer journeys. Marketing starts the process with compelling differentiators, sales validates knee-to-knee, but all sellers carry the process forward: always looking for new value levers (we'll expand this thought process more). The goal of all communication: get the prospect to engage with the value of those outcomes in detail mentally.

- Every customer-facing contributor knows how to reinforce value, especially within their function… and gather intelligence on customer value, "bringing it back to the hive."

- If a company's offerings have sufficient customer-perceived value vs. competing offers, sales result. This obvious, yet crazily underutilized observation is why you've read this far. Even more significantly...

- Profitable sales result when more than "just enough value to win the deal at a discounted price" has been developed. Selling alone is not enough. Your company invests a lot of resources to deliver differentiated customer value and needs to be paid sufficiently if that value premium is to be maintained. Being paid a profitable price for what you provide is the secret sauce in a radically value-focused company.

Price is the Mother's Milk of Profits

Pricing isn't just a number; it should be a corporate capability – a facet of your culture. And, as anyone who has had P&L responsibility can tell you, price is the most powerful lever to profits. And profits fix every problem in your company -- from shareholder value down to a broken coffee maker in a break room.

To simplify the issue of pricing, imagine any piece of business your company recently won. Ask this: "if the price had been either higher or lower, would my company's fulfillment costs have changed in any way?" Most of the time, you would not have negotiated different deliverables but kept the same specified deliverables in the contract. Thus, your costs would be the same under any price/discount level -- and the only two numbers on your income statement that would have changed with a higher or lower price are the revenue line and the profit line.

For those who haven't been seen this in action, I'll quote McKinsey and Company. They found that giving a 1% discount dropped the average Fortune 1000 company's profits by an average of 8%.

A 1% discount drops the average Fortune 1000 company's profits by an average of 8%. ~ McKinsey & Company

That's an average, and it varies inversely with the company's pre-tax profit percentage (I once talked with a low-margin company whose 2.5% pre-tax profits would move by 40% for a 1% change in price).

Now, invert that discount and use the McKinsey average for a price increase. By achieving just a 1% *higher* price, a company's profits increase by an average of 8%. For fun, do a quick value network on what the results of an 8% increase in profits are. Number one bubble on my network: The average CEO can report an 8% increase in profitability during his/her quarterly earnings calls.

For starters, what would an 8% profit increase mean to the company stock price, to the CEO's bonus, to the CSO's compensation, to every salesperson realizing higher sales (and higher gross margins if you've taken my advice to pay them on margin, not revenue)? Next, think of the investments in the business the company can now afford to make to make themselves even more competitive. Now think of impacts on each employee's lives: their career prospects, their immediate vacation plans, their retirement expectations (more compelling than "their retirement accounts"), their ability to pay for kids' colleges and weddings.... you get the idea.

Give me a company's pretax profit percentage, and I can calculate (usually in my head) the percentage change in your profit line. Here's the shortcut: look at your pretax profit percentage. Convert to decimal and take the reciprocal. That's your price leverage factor. For a company with:

   20% pretax profits, the factor is 5.

   15% pretax profits, the factor is 6.67

   10% pretax profits, the factor is 10 (Hypothetical example below)

   5% pretax profits, the factor is 20

Every percent increase in realized price increases your pretax profit by the leverage factor, in percent. For a company at 15% pretax, a 1% effective price increase (increase in price, decrease in discounts given, etc.) will increase profits by 667 basis points; a 2% net pricing increase increases profits by 13.33%, etc.

Price is the Most Powerful Profit Lever, and It's Not Even Close

No other line on your company's income statement has anywhere near the impact on your bottom line as price. The illustration below shows a hypothetical business currently running at 10% pre-tax profit in the left-hand column. The leader of this hypothetical organization wants to increase the company's profits and wants to know where to focus the company's efforts. This comparison shows how much profit "leverage" each line item has by comparing the effects of a 5% change in four different line items. While it's a hypothetical example, doing this same analysis with hundreds of financial statements of real companies yields the same result:

No line on your company's income statement moves profitability more significantly than price does.

	Starting P&L	Increase Volume by 5%	Decrease Sales Exp. 5%	Decrease Fixed Cost 5%	Increase Price by 5%
Revenue	100	105	100	100	105
Variable Costs	40	42	40	40	40
Contrib. Margin	60	63	60	60	65
Sales Expense	6	6	5.7	6	6
Fixed Costs	33	33	33	31.35	33
Gen & Admin Exp.	11	11	11	11	11
Pre-Tax Profit	10	13	10.3	11.65	15
Profit Increase		30%	3%	16.5%	**50%**

Figure 9.1 Profit increase from changing various aspects of a business running at a 10% pretax profit.

Price is the most powerful profit lever, and yet many companies routinely let their salespeople get browbeaten into discounting. In the ultimate demonstration of misplaced priorities, I've actually witnessed salespeople who claim that *it's the company's job to figure out how to make a profit at the price they gave the customer.* On a related note, some sales leaders who let their people discount too easily wonder why they don't have a seat at the management table. Figure 9.1 should begin to tell those sales leaders why.

Some of us train our salespeople to "sell value" and then fail to give them the tools to handle a price discussion successfully. This is snatching defeat out of the jaws of victory. Once you've sold some value, it takes only a little incremental work with the customer to have them quantify it. This is how your customer converts value into a value-based price *that they appreciate, even prefer.*

While it takes a little more work to sell at the right price vs. at a discount, sellers need to do so...every time. Customers want to "get on with it," and sellers do too; every sale without monetizing outcomes is a sale with discounting risk. Remember, as Figure 9.1 shows, no work in your company returns more profit than winning the right price. For that reason, I repeat my call for profit-based sales incentives, as a reinforcement to practice the right behaviors always.

From a management and coaching standpoint, remember that the additional work of building value takes place early during an opportunity pursuit (at least in complex/consensus buying situations). Building value simply consists of asking a couple of pointed value questions throughout the discovery and pursuit process. These questions should be a normal part of helping sellers build the best-fitting solution/offer possible and shouldn't feel unnatural. If those questions aren't asked early, though, they can't be asked late.

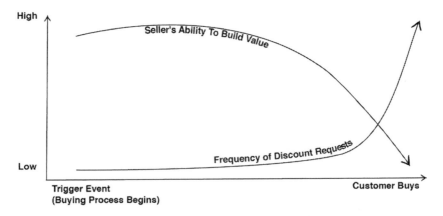

Figure 9.2 Contrast between when value is built vs. when discounting is requested (especially when value was inadequately developed earlier)

Pricing discussions and discounting behaviors tend to occur late in the customer's buying journey. At that point, value-focused questions seem like price-negotiation questions and tend to make customers defensive.

Building a company that provides great customer value takes work, time, and resources. These costs all need to be covered at a long-term profit. The monetary value of an offer must exceed the monetary cost of providing it – that is the purpose of being in business.

Your costs to provide value are none of your customer's business...or your customer's problem.

> Here's a simple thought experiment: If your current price was unprofitable or unsustainable for some reason (other than a transitory one), would your customer increase your price to keep you in business? If the answer is the usual "no," then they aren't concerning themselves with your cost structure (often justifiably). That street needs to go both ways.

As a matter of good customer relations, any request for price reduction should be fairly considered. If your value commands a highly profitable price, and the customer is receiving compelling value, consider any special circumstances that should affect the price. When considering a price reduction, include:

- The value of the outcomes you provide

- The likelihood of substitutes, or equivalent value from others in the future

- How the reduction could improve the relationship with the customer (please don't let the purchasing/procurement department be your source of truth for "improved relationship." More meaningful engagement or no deal).

- If the customer can offer something of comparable value in exchange.

Don't consider:

- Your costs to provide the value you deliver. If the customer is willing to forgo some value and reduce your costs, the magnitude of your cost savings should undoubtedly be considered, but that doesn't mean you should share any figures with a customer.

What is Price?

Let's start by discussing what price *is not*. A pet peeve of mine is (sales) people who disrespect pricing integrity. Price is *not* just another feature of your offer. Price is also not something to be arbitrarily changed when the going gets tough.

Price is also *not* that classic "intersection of the supply and demand curves" you learned about in economics. Classical economic models of supply and demand ignore the way real humans make decisions in the real world. Instead of modeling how people make real decisions, those curves model an artificial way of making decisions that's easier to capture mathematically. Multiple Nobel prizes have been awarded, and an entire branch of economics is built around the difference between what classical economic theory predicts and what really happens.

> *The three basics of behavioral economics (Google the term to learn more): 1) 95% of all decisions are made using mental shortcuts, or heuristics – that defy the mathematical models. 2) Humans filter decisions (it's called framing in the literature) through biases and personal experiences, all of which unduly shape how they see, understand, respond to, and experience the world. 3) Markets have inefficiencies like imperfect information, barriers to entry/exit/switching, emotional decisions, asymmetric negotiating positions, and ability to transfer costs to others without compensation (called externalities)...and at least 20 more...that make the classical mathematical analysis "uninformative" for the value-focused professional.*

Price premium (your price minus the price of the single best option) *is* what your customer weighs against their perception of value (value of your differentiation). This sounds simple, but a customer goes through a lot of mental work before they start making the final price/value tradeoff.

Price declares value. Low price communicates low value, regardless of the real attributes of the product or service. Conversely, humans use high price as an *indicator* of value, even to the point of using price as the basis for assumptions about quality or features. Price and perceived value reinforce one another in a loop. For this reason alone, you cannot afford to think of price as a feature; discounting can pollute the perceived value of every other feature.

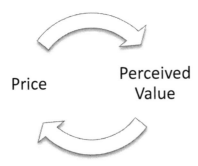

Figure 9.3 Price is shaped by value, but also declares your value

Salespeople often forget that their price negotiations reflect on the overall perceived value of the brand they represent.

> Macy's used to be a high-end retailer, but no longer. It lowered its own brand image through rack after rack of heavily discounted clothing until consumers got the message that Macy's clothes are not high-end; they are just ordinary. The phrase "hoisted on their own petard" comes to mind here.

Lower price reduces the perception of the quality, which starts the proverbial "race to the bottom."

Most business professionals understand all of this, but the trick is to give your sellers the tools to have win-win value vs. pricing conversations with your customers. To facilitate these value discussions, such tools need to be easy to understand, use, teach, coach, and reinforce.

It turns out that the language of value we've been presenting throughout this book is the basis of those pricing conversations (I know...surprise!). Translating demonstrated customer value to pricing – and profitability – should become part of the company's operating rhythm. Quantifying the value you've developed in your "deep and wide" value hunting process is an essential aspect of Full Value Selling™.

Harnessing the Customer's Decision Process

Any selling process should align with a customer buying process to be effective. Aligning with the customer value/pricing evaluation process is no different. The price/value discussion I present in this book mirrors the most common "decision heuristic" (mental buying process) described in consumer choice research. Because it is what buyers use most often, it is more intuitive and comfortable.

Remember from chapter 2 that customers use decision whatever processes seem the most efficient: "the human mind devises efficient ways to get on with things." The usual choice rules are to narrow options down quickly – using rapid elimination methods – to a final two options, and then perform a more detailed comparison between the last two. This process isn't good or bad; it's just what humans usually do. A value-focused organization simply needs to harness human behavior rather than fight it.

Those who have been involved in a "final three" situation with bids, RFPs, or the like: behind closed doors, or at least within the minds of those involved in the buying decision, this "rapid elimination down to the final two" behavior is still the norm. My theory is that when a group decision is involved, the group's final three almost always encompasses every individual group member's final two.

To make the finalist list, you need to harness the human principle of immediacy (also called the availability heuristic). The criteria used for early eliminations are those most immediately "available," or mentally recalled at the moment. Embedding differentiators deeply in a customer's mind makes it easier for them to recall...and use. The value-building process builds a detailed mental value picture that's easy to recall. Recall from chapter 2: evaluating, extending, expanding, and then calculating value of differentiators forces them to build a detailed internal story (salespeople are also welcome to tell applicable success stories, an effective sales technique) around differentiators. *This detail makes a differentiator easier to recall.* When the time comes for a buying group to make a decision, that story will carry considerable weight in the buying decision.

> *As decisions become more formalized and documented, it's also a best practice to try to influence the process steps and/or decision process. Driving a group toward the process, they'd be most comfortable with informally is an easy sell.*

The Value Balance

A common decision algorithm that most humans utilize is the one harnessed in Full Value Selling™. Aligning with this thought process means aligning with a heuristic your customer uses and is comfortable with.

As buyers, once we have narrowed the choices down to the final two, we compare differences. At the final choice stage, we ignore similarities and even unimportant differences (remember, you've been making your differences as important as possible through the entire sales process by developing value).

Consumers put your offer's price difference on one side of an internal scale. In the drawing below, the price premium is measured in dollars and cents, and thus easy to weigh precisely. The left side of the scale below is measurable in objectively – outside the customer's mind. The right side of the scale is different. Value drivers are held up next to the scale, but not put on the scale. This is because the customer has agreed to them (thus put them on their internal scale) but hasn't given them a specific weight. Customers won't voluntarily expend the mental effort to weigh each accurately – unless they need to. If the driver(s) looks like it will outweigh the real-world price premium, the customer will buy.

As drawn, the fuzzy balls look too light to this buyer, who will conclude that the price premium isn't justified. The right side is filled with business outcomes, personal outcomes, logical justifications, and emotional ones. Don't leave out any.

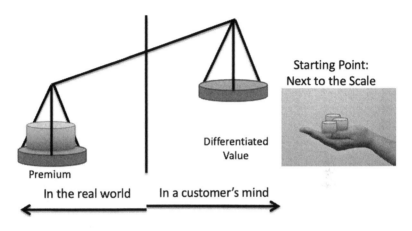

Figure 9.4 The value balance, with value drivers inadequately understood, but only vaguely visualized by a customer.

All of my professional life, I've worked with products and services with a price premium. From early on in my career, I was taught to help the client examine and weigh each differentiator. Through my experience, "held up beside the scale" drivers – customer estimates of value -- always gain weight after customer examination, which is why sellers need to guide customers through an examination process. *Fully developed value* has always weighed more than vague value. Here is a simple example:

> I am indifferent between the styling of my two new car finalists, the Lincoln vs. its Ford equivalent (they're actually built on the same platform, meaning differences are almost entirely cosmetic and brand cachet): the price difference is $7400. But I want the leather seat option and upgraded sound system: standard on the Lincoln, optional on the Ford (I am indifferent to the other differences the Lincoln offers), which brings the real difference to $4000. I don't know the difference in resale value, don't care to research it, and won't trust the salesperson's figures, so, like most consumers, I will value it at zero, since it seems so far in the future, so uncertain, and so difficult to educate myself on. Let's say that the Lincoln carries free oil changes and scheduled maintenance, which is worth $1000/year to me in saved time and hassle. Thus, If I plan to keep the car for four years, I am exactly at the indifference point between the two, and whoever discounts their option (changes the price premium) wins.

> If I carry clients around in my vehicle (say, if I'm a Realtor), I may predict that the Lincoln brand cachet will communicate success – emotional value. But buyers rationalize emotional value in business terms. If that results in even one additional client per year...which is worth $15,000/yr in commission

income to me; the premium purchase is a no-brainer based upon this value alone. If the Lincoln salesman hadn't uncovered that aspect, he might have needed to discount to move me off of the indifference point.

Throughout the discovery and positioning process, sellers need to uncover personal and business (emotional and logical) differentiators which deliver value to the customer, and to get the customer to measure that value monetarily – at the very minimum, discuss the outcome impacts (both business and personal) in as much detail as possible.

The $15,000/year "more customers/more income" value premium in the example is something that every seller needs to understand – especially if you aren't ever going to sell me a car. This type of value proposition is one of the "unconventional, but predictably recurring" layers of value I discussed in the last chapter. The car salesperson in the example won't sell only to realtors – or even to the types of professionals where the same type of "increased revenue" calculation applies. A great car salesman should always ask a prospect about lifestyle and job during discovery (early in the sales process) to help them pick the right vehicle. This information also happens to be useful when the inevitable discussion of price vs. competing alternatives comes up. Note: It won't matter that many other vehicles also promise this particular "projects success, drives more revenue" image. Those other vehicles aren't in this customer's final two: they've been eliminated for other reasons and are unlikely to be considered at all.

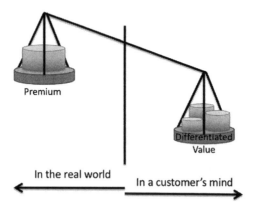

Figure 9.5 The value balance, with value drivers fully quantified by a customer.

Buyers choose the most direct mental path to a conclusion. This means that they will only monetize a differentiator if they need to (or if the salesperson guides them through the process). If a quick approximation of the value will support their decision adequately, that's what they use. If the value balance looks close to even, people will often figure that either way is fine rather than actually mentally digging into the details.

When the value scale looks even, the status quo/do nothing looks more attractive.

*If the value scales look close to evenly balanced **within a group's** buying decision dynamic, it becomes riskier for one of the group to step forward and champion a favorite. If a seller can help add significant "weight" to the value side of the balance, however, a champion becomes easier to recruit.*

In the car example, the $1000/yr in "included service" sounds like a high number until the seller makes the customer calculate the number of oil changes and service appointments, then the time sitting in a dealer waiting room, then hourly productivity costs. If the seller promises a free loaner car or Uber reimbursement (not the dealer's annoying shuttle service) so the customer can get back to work while the car is being serviced, that $1000/year of value can be pretty easy to get to for a professional buyer, but probably not for a minimum wage earner (again, a recurring-but-not-universal value proposition that a seller should be aware of well before price negotiations start in earnest).

The diagram below introduces the basic arithmetic of full value. Starting with the price of the single best option or SBO, the competitor weighs advantages of the SBO, and differentiators of your option.

The single best option is the next best choice to your offer. This could include "stick with the status quo/do nothing," "build it myself," or any other option. Remember, humans quickly narrow down to the final two, then start doing detailed thinking like this. There is little need to do this calculation for multiple "next best choices," given how humans make decisions.

Sellers must help them develop value all the way to full monetization of all differentiators – direct, indirect, and personal. After all of the dollars are subtracted and added, the result is "The Full Value Price." At this price, the customer would be indifferent to you vs. the competitor, because you have charged them a price equal to all of the value they would receive when buying from you.

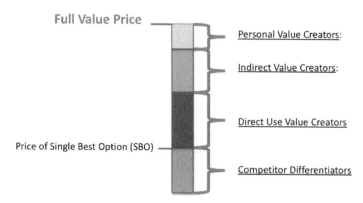

Figure 9.6 How full value is calculated.

This approach mimics the most common buying heuristic (mental process) that human beings use when making buying decisions. Complicated ROI calculators add detail but are not as intuitive. Worse, they are subject to a drawn-out "battle of the underlying assumptions" between the buying and selling organization. The simple approach tends to avoid that, giving a buyer a clear, intuitive, comfortable buying justification, using all the same factors that would have gone into an ROI spreadsheet.

The Value Calculator - Translating Customer Value Discussions to Price Discussions

Inevitably, a selling organization needs to put pricing in place for an opportunity, a product/service, or a market. These decisions always require one critical input: "what is it worth to a buyer"? Most companies use approximate answers. Value-focused companies can answer this question with higher precision.

> *Value, since it's always in the customer mind, is difficult to measure with "precision." When done properly, the value calculator drives sellers to articulate a "much more precise" measurement of customer perceived value.*

The Value Analysis captures the monetized value of every value driver. Here is a simplified version, for the car example above...specifically for the Lincoln salesperson and the Realtor prospect.

Differentiator	Outcome and Value	Monetized Value
Better Service Logistics	20 hours/year saved from waiting area	$1000/yr x 4 yr
Higher Resale Value?	Not able to establish value	$0
Additional amenities	Customer acknowledged, but neutral	Tiebreaker?
Lincoln projects Successful image	At least one more Real Estate transaction/yr	$15,000/yr
(Mgr Note): Business Expense deduction.	Entire amount, including additional $4,000, is tax-deductible.	Let's brainstorm how to address

Figure 9.5 A basic value calculator, AKA, the full value analysis.

As detailed information is gathered, it becomes part of a Full Value Analysis/calculator. First, proposed differentiators are entered into the left column; these are value hypotheses. As a differentiator is *validated with the prospect*, results are recorded and tracked in the middle column of the value analysis worksheet. Finally, the *customer-calculated measurement* of that value is recorded on the right column -- in complex sales, there will be a column the persona who values each outcome. The auto example is for a single persona, so that part of the analysis worksheet is missing in the example above.

The value analysis summarizes every differentiator/value driver in play for the opportunity and captures *the customer calculated value.* Value exists in the customer's mind, so analysis, calculations, and dollarized value must be in customer terms.

Always remember that the value analysis always has two levels of imprecision: it's our estimate of the customer's perception. Great sales conversation skills and methodologies --combined with rigorous value discipline-- help sellers squeeze some imprecision out (I have personally worked these value analyses down to the penny with customers), but you should always be mindful of that potential error. More discussion on this point later.

You will see that all of the differentiators discussed with the prospect are listed, even the "higher resale value" with a zero value, and the "additional amenities" the Lincoln offers (such as a few additional cupholders, and more woodgrain plastic on the dashboard). This helps us confirm what discussion have already/have not yet happened, and what results of any conversations are. This allows for both team selling collaboration and better manager coaching.

Value analysis supports team selling. As this analysis was shared with colleagues or brought up during a team sales meeting, colleagues could help come up with new approaches, and/or gain insights from a different angle or using different personas. For instance, somebody in the used car or fleet area could help the salesperson craft an approach to the trade-in value issue, to see if the customer could develop some value there. In other industries, team collaboration on the value analysis can be extremely powerful.

> Example: After a sales engineer uncovers cost avoidance in our offer's software upgrade path, and defines that value with the customer's IT group, our sales engineer should enter a new "upgrade cost avoidance" line on the value analysis for that sales opportunity.

Coaching sales teams using the value analysis is a powerful way to reinforce and develop successful behaviors. In the value analysis above, a manager suggested a new value source. Since this buyer will be using the vehicle for business, the vehicle investment may tax-deductible for this customer. The manager notes this gap in the analysis and offers to walk the seller through the complexities of tax deductibility on a purchase vs. lease, and how to NOT go so far as to give tax advice.

The total value premium that the customer has calculated is $64,000 (4 years x $15K plus 4x $1K), far more than the price of the vehicle. If the customer balks at 1-2 sales a year, the seller can fall back to 1/year, and then all the way to "just one more sale during the life of the car," and the purchase price premium of $4,000 is still covered. As the seller gains confidence in what actual calculation the customer is using, they can hold to their existing offered price (without any further discounting) with greater confidence. For the realtor customer, the tiebreakers don't even come into play. For a non-realtor, they might, depending on what additional value is uncovered.

> *In this example, there is also the threat of losing the customer to another Lincoln dealer for the same exact model. Once the Lincoln is established in the customer's mind as the choice, the "next best choice" shifts to "identical model/different dealership." While important in the car example, let's ignore it for now, please.*

For salespeople, value discipline gives the confidence to know that their premium price is justified – even a bargain. It gives them the basis to have a productive conversation with any buying persona, even that purchasing agent who reflexively blurts, "Your price is too high." It gives buyers a value calculation that they can use to justify your pricing to themselves. Finally, the exercise of having quantified the value to themselves increases their preference for your product/service at a higher price. Here's an example:

> A salesperson who sold software to municipalities shared his situation and the pricing he'd quoted a certain city. The city currently operated a home-grown software package for printing utility bills, and the two employees who had written the code were retiring. They had offered to support part of the existing system as paid consultants, but not the interfaces to other software packages, and the city was deciding between this option and my client's software. The salesperson had quoted the system with 25% of "negotiating

room." That is, he could drop from his quoted price by 25% before even asking for a pricing exception from his management.

As we prepared him to discuss just how much of that 25% he would really need to sacrifice, we developed a value analysis. This analysis included the costs of the external consultant fees, additional costs of maintaining the "non-covered" interfaces, the costs of manual data entry of thousands of meter readings every month, the costs of correcting keystroke errors from that manual data entry, the costs of having to apologize to the mayor and city council members for ongoing problems (strongly hinting at job risk, which would appear on somebody's *personal* value analysis, but nowhere else), etc. The salesperson had already identified these costly outcomes with the customer but had not quantified them monetarily. Using our own rough estimates, it turned out that the Full Value of the software package was ***three times*** what was quoted.

There was no way the quote could be – or should be – increased to its full value. The salesperson did agree, though, that he no longer felt he would need to discount off of his currently quoted premium price once he could help his customer calculate value for themselves. He left our meeting with true pricing courage, and even better, with a plan for conversations to help his customer become excited about the cost savings (vs. the alternative) they would realize at his full price.

This single coaching conversation about a single customer opportunity more than they paid for my entire consulting engagement with them.

This example shows one but hints at the second use of full value pricing analysis. Those two uses:

1. Using full value analysis to **hold to standard pricing** for a standard product.

2. **Setting price** for a custom or semi-custom product.

The first is by far the most common and is worth the effort it takes to build value-based pricing as a corporate capability.

Run the numbers for how much your company provided in the way of discounts last year, and then estimate how many of those discount dollars you probably didn't need to give up. Because every dollar discounted is a profit dollar, calculate what would happen if you showed that much more profitable revenue last year...to the company, your workers, your sellers, your stock price, executive bonuses, etc. What would it be worth to build value discipline into your organization simply from the standpoint of pricing? See the value analysis I just did there?

Full Value Selling Breaks Old Assumptions About Demand Curves – It Builds Preference at a Higher Price

A lot of readers will have alarms going off inside their heads at this point, thinking, "if I raise my prices (or discount less), the law of demand says I'll drive away customers." I don't buy it. The law of demand you are invoking describes an imaginary buyer, "homo economicus." [43] Real buyers don't see all competing offers as identical substitutes (at least not when your sellers are doing it right.)

Building a value analysis with the customer – getting *their* valuation of each differentiator and outcome – is the practice of building a concrete justification for your offer. Building value inside the customer's mind builds preference, which can build loyalty. As a matter of fact, buyer preference for your solution can be "measured" as full value price minus actual price.

> The difference between preference, a decision-time phenomenon, and loyalty, a long-term measure, is how accurately the value analysis tracks to the experienced result. Woe to the seller who fails to deliver on promised value.

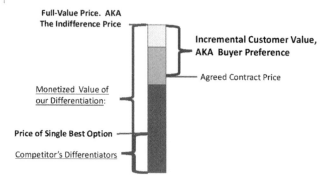

Figure 9.7 Calculating buyer preference from the full value price

Full Value Selling as a Way of Life.

While there are selling behaviors to master, the math is pretty simple. If you have a value premium for the customer, they are likely to choose your offer. *If the competitor shifts the balance by dropping the price (thus increasing your price premium,* your value premium remains, but is added to a lower SBO.

> In both the Lincoln vs. Ford and the software examples above, the full value premium was so high that the opportunity was discount-proof: a competitor couldn't overcome the value premium by giving their product or service away.

---

[43] Homo economicus, or "econs" for short, is the term academic economists use to describe the artificial person whose behavior mimics an economic supply/demand model. Behavioral economists like Nobel laureates Richard Thaler (read any of his books, and you'll want to read them all), Amos Tversky and Tversky's colleague Daniel Kahneman (who would have shared Tversky's Nobel if he was still alive) can describe those differences in convincing detail. This book is meant to translate those differences into actionable tools and practices for the business professional.

These selling outcomes only became possible when sellers developed Full Value in the customer's mind. In the software situation (the one that really happened), the salesperson started our session under the assumption that he was going to need to discount, and just wanted help figuring out how deeply.

There are a few other advantages that go to the seller who gets the prospect to perform a detailed analysis:

1. You harness the power of the immediacy principle: the more detailed their analysis, the more detailed the story they tell themselves about the outcomes associated with choosing your offer. Thus, the more likely they will be to recall it at decision time, and therefore,

2. The more heavily they will weigh it.

3. The value of a differentiator almost always rises as sellers develop value with customers. Preference rises and can be measured by the difference between your offered price and their calculated value.

During an opportunity pursuit, all sellers, as part of a team selling effort, should collaboratively assemble a full value analysis. Initially, the search for differentiators is guided by value networks. Most sales methodologies help organize personas in a complex sale but aren't strong on suggesting new ones. Value networks often identify a larger group of value-impacted parties – they complement opportunity methodologies by adding depth (that third dimension: value) to an opportunity pursuit.

One key to remember: humans prefer their decision processes simple. You need to build all the value you will ever need before buying decision time. After that, it's hard for either you or a competitor to go back and add new differentiators to the value balance – adjustments other than price become increasingly difficult. Neither you nor your competitor can easily add differentiators at the late stage – and it's even more challenging to get the prospect to monetize them. The goal is to have discount-proof value going into the customer's final decision. As we talked about earlier, the difficulty of getting another bite at the value apple is one major reason selling to *Full Value* is different from many "value selling" methodologies.

Finding Home Run Value – Making Your Offer Mission-Critical

When an outcome from your product/service impacts a top management priority -- in any meaningful way – it's possible that your offer is promoted to *mission-critical* status. When that happens, the sales conversation becomes elevated to senior levels in an organization. This isn't as rare as many salespeople think it is. Selling to full value helps.

In my experience, when one of your differentiators gives the customer a competitive advantage *with its customers (i.e., with your customer's customer)*, you have potentially game-ending (discount-proof, competitor-proof) value.

The monetary value of increased revenue or competitiveness is often much higher than the entire cost of your offer (again, look at the Lincoln buying Realtor). The biggest question in monetizing such an outcome is how to make that advantage real to the customer and getting them to estimate the full value.

As nearly as possible, sellers should quantify *every* possible point of differentiation, then sum them together to determine *Full Value* (the value calculator). It's seldom possible to completely uncover Full Value in the real selling world. Thus, Full Value is aspirational in practice. But as anyone who has lost to a last-minute competitive discount understands, selling to Full Value is also an imperative.

Full Value Probably Isn't the Same as Your Price

Once Full Value (or as close to it as you can get) is calculated, the seller can decide where to set the price. Assuming that your estimate of the customer's perception is perfect, Full Value Price represents the competitor's price plus the monetary value of all of your differentiators. If you were to charge Full Value as your price, the customer would be theoretically indifferent...or you would be relying on the tiebreakers plus any unknown value you'd missed. Offering one dollar under that Full Value price means giving them one dollar's worth of motivation to choose you.

We price at some amount less than full value for a few reasons.

- First, we want a safety margin for the imprecision of our estimate of Full Value.

- Second, and most important: we want to provide motivation to buy. Full value minus price offered equals *incremental customer value* or buyer preference.

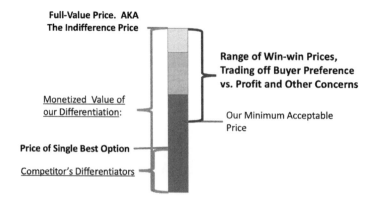

Figure 9.8 Going from the full-value price to a win-win selling price.

Other things equal, higher incremental customer value (larger gap between Full Value and price offered) translates into higher buying preference. Buyer motivation and buyer preference for your offer are synonymous. As your offer delivers the promised value (post-purchase), buyer preference turns into customer loyalty.

Once Full Value (or as close to it as you can get) is calculated, the seller can decide where to set the price – or how much/whether to discount. In the case of products with standard pricing, setting the price isn't the issue; successfully resisting discounting from regular price is the issue. For other opportunities, price setting involves balancing multiple factors:

1. Confidence in the calculation of Full Value (remember, these numbers are often *our estimate of the customer's perception.* Full Value is always subject to some imprecision, and pricing below full value absorbs estimation risk.

2. Threat of competitors. A high enough price can be an incentive for new entrants. I have talked to more than one client who wants to charge enough profit to live, but not so much to attract any new competitors. This is a great motivation, but cementing your full value into a customer's mind is at very least an effective second layer of "competitor deterrent."

   If these are big, important customers that you can't afford to lose, you should be building (and trying to expand) full value regardless of your pricing strategy.

3. Size of the premium. Even if the price is defensible based upon calculated value, a large price premium creates a perception that needs to be managed purposely. If you're perceived as gouging, you might achieve a short-term win that was really a long-term loss[44].

   More than one pricing consulting firm whose fee is based upon a percentage of price increases has put their client into this bind. Unfortunately, the pricing consultant is long gone before the long-term damage shows up.

4. Strategic considerations. Is pricing one of the tools in the relationship management strategy, or is there some other strategic reason to set a win-win price at a specific level?

These considerations sound complicated and possibly troublesome to some. I suppose they are more complex and troublesome than winging it. Having the information to make robust pricing decisions is unfamiliar territory to many.

---

[44] Martin Skreli, the "pharma bro" makes a good case study.

Utilizing value analysis helps organizations operate with clearer insights, enabling better decisions.

Full Value Isn't Always a Premium Price – Supporting Robust Discounting Decisions

Full value represents the maximum a customer is willing to pay...at least to within the confidence range of your estimate of the customer's perception of value. The value in the customer's mind is the value...all of it. Wanting more value than is there isn't going to make it appear. Your choices are "build more value" or "live with what's there." It sometimes happens that customer value is less than the seller's minimum acceptable price:

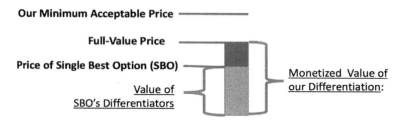

Figure 9.9 An illustration of full value less than the minimum acceptable price.

When a sales opportunity doesn't show sufficient value to price profitably, it's time to decide:

- How deeply to discount. It may not be as much as we would have thought before implementing full value discipline. Value analysis should be **required** as part of *every* pricing exception request. No value calculator (and no coaching and validation of that value calculation), no discounts. No exceptions.

- Can we change the offer, reducing our cost by more than it reduces customer value? Customer conversations about this possibility can often uncover value neither of you was aware of previously.

- Can we pull some of our costs out of this transaction that renders this opportunity acceptable? Your value analysis should point you toward some likely candidates.

- Do we accept contribution pricing? That is, do we price below fully allocated cost (variable costs plus the regular allocation of fixed/overhead costs), but above variable costs? The road to business failure is paved with marginally priced opportunities, so use caution. You'll go broke if these are the only deals you win, but more profitable if you consume *unused capacity* with deals that "soak up" some fixed costs, even if it's below their "normal" share. If you're operating above breakeven, these are decisions about utilizing unused capacity. If you're below breakeven, they may be short-term survival decisions.

If marginally priced business makes it impossible to capture more profitable business, make sure you won't regret it.

- o If we do, how do we manage expectations inside the company?
- o If we do, how do we keep this piece of business from polluting our entire customer base?

In many businesses, people join new companies, carrying the knowledge of discounts along with them. In other businesses, customers talk. There is no such thing as an isolated pricing decision.

- Do we walk away? This option is hard to consider in the moment. A marginally priced opportunity consumes our capacity and limits our ability to pursue more profitable business. I've absolutely seen situations where respectfully declining the business is best for the customer relationship.

Letting a competitor fail at an unprofitable price is often a better strategy than it might seem in the moment. There are some customers that you do wish on your rivals.

Is better business out there somewhere? If so, what's keeping us from it? If not, what do we do about profitably capturing the business that we can capture? These are difficult questions, made even tougher by the resources that have already been invested in the opportunity pursuit. A complete value analysis will help both you and the customer understand if and why disengaging is the best course.

Building Profits via a Rigorous Pricing and Discounting Process

One of the sales operations areas I focus on with clients is their discounting, or "pricing exceptions" process. Every dollar discounted to a customer isn't just a revenue dollar; it's a profit dollar. Developing rigor around how and when you give profit dollars to your customers is one of those "home run value" pursuits I engage in with my clients. Annual discounting dollars are typically orders of magnitude higher than I could ever charge. They are also the basis for the highly profitable "shared gains" business model of many pricing consultancies.

> *While a contingency-based fee, or "shared profits" from repricing your company's offers may seem appealing, the divergence in incentives argues for caution. If your consultant gets paid on a share of short-term price gains, they have a perverse incentive to get you to price at long-term customer alienation levels. I discussed this in another footnote, but it bears repeating.*

Companies who implement Full Value Selling have a more solid basis for making discounting decisions, as I just explored above. Value-focused companies build robust pricing exceptions processes. A Value Analysis/calculator is the price of entry; no value analysis, no pricing exception. No exceptions.

Without good value discipline, companies allocate discount dollars erratically. Their "system" can look something like directing discounts toward:

- The salesperson who is best at gaming the price exception process.

- The lousy salesperson that management feels sorriest for.

- The salesperson with the best excuses or the most irritating voice.

- Customers with the most bluster, or who know the president's phone number.

- Most desperate sales manager.

- Sales manager (or their VP of Sales. Or their CEO looking forward to the next earnings call. Let's be honest) who thinks that this month's low-profit bookings are better than next month's high-profit bookings...

I am thrilled to help readers of this book to analyze where their discount dollars go and their system for allocating those dollars. Some of the questions we'll probably go through:

- How many discount dollars do you spend per year?

   o Formal, through an exception process?
   o Invisible, through salesperson autonomy?
   o Does everyone in your company know that discount dollars=profit dollars? Do they act like it?

- What is your price exception/discount process now?

   o What are the steps?
   o Who are the players?
   o What information/documentation is used?
   o How is customer value measured/characterized? How is the discount justified?
   o Do you always know what the customer thinks of yours and the competitor's value (or just their price)?

- How consistently is your pricing exception process followed?

- Have you (or can we) analyze how discount dollars are distributed? Are there concentrations by: territory/salesperson, region, customer, industry, time of year? Can we explain any apparent anomalies?

- What have we gotten in return for price concessions? Are there any salesperson/regional/market trends in that data?

If you have a solid methodology for understanding customer value, some great things happen to your discounting practices:

- Discounting is purposeful. It no longer feels as random or arbitrary.

    o Your people will understand the system and feel more fairly treated
    o You might quiet the squeaky wheels, the people who scream the loudest for discounts.

- You have confidence in your discounting decisions.

    o You'll make better decisions about product enhancements, market entries, even market exits.

- You will discount less and profit more.

- Your forecasts will become more accurate. Knowing customer value is the same as knowing customer motivation, and you are intimately involved in the customer's innermost buying decision dynamics.

There is almost nothing you can do in your business with a higher financial payback than getting your arms around your discounting practices and putting value-based discipline around your pricing exceptions policy and processes.

I mentioned it earlier, but it bears repeating: Your sales compensation/reward system needs to align with the practices in selling value. If your sellers are compensated on revenue, you'll get revenue. If they are rewarded for profitable revenue, you'll get that, especially if you give them the skills to understand and build value.

Pricing Games People Play

It should be noted there are some customers who insist on keeping vendors at a more "controllable," commoditized level to increase negotiating leverage, etc. Those customers may be manipulating you. Some devalue your contribution for the purpose of negotiation. One sign that this may be happening: limiting communication to various stakeholders.

Another dynamic that isn't a purposeful game but is just as dangerous: the low-value loop we discussed earlier. When salespeople don't conduct compelling, enlightening value conversations, they are seen as unremarkable, and not worth engaging with. Customers self-educate, then put out highly specific, often unimaginative, bid packages. Unremarkable sellers respond directly to those bids, never uncovering additional or unconventional value, which reinforces the impression that salespeople aren't worth engaging with...and the loop continues. This is the "multiple business cards, but all selling the same thing" problem, reinforcing itself. Your entire company, from marketing messages, to sellers, to technical experts, needs to break that cycle by adding unconventional value at every opportunity.

It's prevalent in certain industries to enforce a "quiet period" around a bid, RFP, or similar purchasing event. Understanding how value tentacles spread through a prospect and how important it is to develop all of that value, the old advice to "get in front of an RFP" takes on even more urgency. A best practice is to evaluate any unexpected RFP as a no-bid candidate. The rules for no-bidding and/or asking for additional access to buying personas are worth a chapter in themselves. I'm not sure I could do any better than Tom Williams and Tom Saine treated precisely this topic in their book *The Seller's Challenge*[45].

I'd also like to give a shout-out to those customers who don't ever want to pay a fair price. Other things being equal, these are less valuable customers; they often:

- Consume an inappropriate share of your resources,
- Demand more management attention,
- Insist on less profitable pricing,
- Demand free or underpriced exceptions like product changes and expedites
- Refuse to take their share of any blame for (much less pay the price for) miscommunication
- (in my experience) tend to be more interruptive,
- Alienate your customer service people disproportionately,
- Can be some of the slowest payers,
- Spread the need to discount to all of your other customers
- ...and more.

I can't tell you unequivocally to fire these customers, but I am duty-bound as your value advisor to ask you to make a more purposeful calculation of the value flowing each way in such relationships. I can also suggest that raising

---

[45] The Seller's Challenge. How Top Sellers Master 10 Deal Killing Obstacles in B2B Sales. Thomas Williams, Thomas Saine, Strategic Dynamincs inc. ISBN: 9781948974028

prices to customers you wouldn't mind losing can turn them into better customers.

Valuable Bonus: More Accurate Forecasts!

Knowing customer value with precision closes a lot of operational loops in a selling organization. One of the most important is forecast accuracy.

Let face it. Forecasting is a fancy name for predicting the future. It will always be uncertain. The object of good sales forecasting is understanding the uncertainties and incorporating them into business prediction.

Knowing customer value down to dollars and cents (or whatever your local currency is) minus your price equals the incremental value received by the customer; it's a measure of buyer preference for your solution. Knowing incremental customer value with precision does wonders for your forecasting acumen. If you want to predict what each customer will do in the future, a great starting point is knowing monetarily how they compare their options.

Measuring motivation is not something most companies can incorporate into their forecasting. Value-focused companies can do so with relative ease.

Bottom line: forecasts informed by an understanding of the customer's innermost buying decision dynamics are going to be much more accurate than those without.

Key Take-Aways

Corporate Leaders: If profits are the one most important thing you need to produce, your company needs to be able to price to the value your company provides. Price is the strongest lever to increase profits. In my experience, price is the one area your salespeople could most dramatically and most rapidly change your profitability.

Sales Leaders: An orderly language of value gives you the ability to price effectively. Analyze where your discounting dollars go. Do they go to some salespeople more than others? Are you sure your price exception system isn't throwing discount dollars at the squeakiest wheels?

Many companies need a more rational system for making pricing and discounting decisions. The foundation of any such system is knowing—really knowing – how much your customer thinks your offer is worth to them. If you can coach your team in understanding and developing full value, they'll be more successful

This chapter also opens the door to more accurate forecasts. Incremental customer value is the most powerful insight into customer likelihood to buy there is.

Sales coaching should also be easier. Value calculators are the aggregation of performing a lot of sales behaviors well. Coach value calculations, and you are focusing on the highest value selling behaviors.

You may also need to fix a problem with sales compensation. I will repeat my call for a profitability-based reward system. Don't let the difficulty of getting super-accurate profitability estimates hold you back. A famous statistician, quant jock, and possible inventor of the computer terms "bit" and "byte," John Tukey once said: "Far better an approximate answer to the right question than a precise answer to the wrong question." Your goal is incentivizing the right behaviors, not reporting profits perfectly

Sales Enablement Leaders: An orderly language of value gives you the ability to enable effectively. Value calculators make sales coaching easier. Rather than monitoring behaviors in role-plays, ride-alongs, or interpreting them from meeting plans and call reports, you can directly coach the outcomes of value-oriented selling behaviors. To assemble and calculate a great estimate of the customer's perception, a seller has to do a lot of things right...and they're all the right things for a sales enablement pro to measure.

Discipline around discounting also becomes much more objective. Many organizations treat access to discounting as a black art mastered by a select few sellers. Now discounting can be around objective measures – measures which you can train, track, coach, and manage. They also help bridge gaps between marketing and product organizations, by helping to have solid, objective measures of the value of differentiators you offer or could offer.

Sales Operations Leaders: A value calculator form should become a crucial part of your sales operations toolset. If you are involved in discounting or a pricing exceptions process, they will become the central point of focus.

If you are involved in sales compensation, I will repeat the call for profitability-based reward systems. I know that in many companies, internal accounting/costing makes accurate profit calculation almost impossible. In this case, I invoke John Tukey's (famous statistician, quant jock, and possible inventor of the computer terms "bit" and "byte") quote: "Far better an approximate answer to the right question than a precise answer to the wrong question." The goal is incentivizing the right behavior, not reporting profits perfectly.

Sellers: Selling Full Value isn't "extra work." It's building a more powerful sales strategy—to win more deals more comfortably. It's building a wall against competitive threats. It also means knowing how – and how much your prospect values your offer. The idea of full value also gives you guidance to gain consensus within a complex sale.

If that value is not enough to support your price, you'll know it. You'll be able to make sound pricing decisions and make objective, fact-based discounting recommendations, not just feeling-based.

Finally, your forecasts will be more fact-based rather than feelings-based...and more accurate.

Marketing Professionals: By examining value analyses from sellers, you will be learning what outcomes are most compelling to your organization's customers and will be able to market to those outcomes more compellingly. Value analysis is persona-based, so your ABM materials will also benefit. Correspondingly, value analysis also informs the creation of more targeted sales training materials.

Product/Service Professionals: By examining value analyses from sellers, you will be learning what outcomes are most compelling to your organization's customers, and will gain insight into use cases and customer applications. I have found that this informs more value focused (and more profitable) innovation. As you participate in product training, you'll be able to communicate customer outcomes and value much more clearly. Equipping sellers to look for value gaps your offer can fill is elite product training.

Part
FIVE

Are You Ready to be Radical?

In part one, we made a case for the Radically Value Focused organization. In part two, we assembled an understanding of value from research in psychology, behavioral economics, and consumer behavior -- all to help you understand how value develops inside the customer's mind. Part three explored basic business acumen for everyone in an organization (something many in modern business is sorely lacking), but especially those in customer-facing roles need to have insightful business discussions that position them as valued advisors. Part four proposes a set of tools, to be combined with sales skills and methodologies (as appropriate) to uncover, develop, and sell to a "deep and wide" understanding of all of the value your offer has to your customers.

In the final part of this book, I want to revisit the value-focused enterprise in more detail. We'll start by describing the value-focused company, department by department, one chapter for sellers (all customer-facing roles), then another for all of the functions supporting sales[46]. We'll occasionally compare it to "for-profit" and "for process" companies. Then I'll talk about the behavior coaching involved in making the shift. Finally, I'll close the book with some topics on implementation and change management.

---

[46] This is an homage to Michael Houlihan and Bonnie Harvey, founders of Barefoot Wines. In The Barefoot Spirit, their NYT best seller, they explained that that Barefoot was organized into two departments: Sales, and Sales Support. Michael Houlihan and I spent a few enjoyable moments in 2018 mind-melding on what I call "building a business from the customer in".

Chapter
TEN

Enabling All Sellers to Focus on Value

Value focus isn't just *pitching* value, because you can't sell value without knowing how your customer sees value. We usually think of sales as the owner of the customer-information-gathering experience...but that view is sagging under the weight of increasing involvement of more and more "non-sales" groups...customer service, tech support, technical sales, implementation, and customer satisfaction...the list goes on. Sales "owns" the customer relationship less and less. In this book, I've used the word "sellers" to describe anyone who touches the customer, with an eye toward de-siloing all of these roles.

This chapter is devoted to understanding how much information flows into your company and developing a more robust way of capturing that information. We'll walk through the entire arc of the customer experience, examining the types of information that can come in through each channel. The goal is not just to have everybody pitch in to gather intelligence on customer value, bringing it back to the hive; it's so everybody knows how to build value with customers.

While value focus is a company-wide discipline, sellers – again, any of the specialized roles that consistently touch the customer -- still carry the bulk of the value discovery and characterization burden. Coaching value discipline is similarly a company-wide effort, but sellers are a focal point.

Training on value discipline is like any other training that requires behavior change: follow-up sustainment, reinforcement, and coaching is required to ensure adoption.

As I coach clients through sales improvement implementations, we add the elements of value focus to gain clarity on what is happening in the customer's journey. This way, sales can execute on the mission of leveraging customer value into won opportunities. It usually becomes apparent that all customer-contacting roles need to join in.

Figure 10.1 A repeat of figure 3.2 Value focus adds depth to the entire hierarchy of organizational sales acumen

The diagram above was first introduced in Chapter 2, to highlight how important coaching is in the development of robust sales capability, and then how *value focus* gives all of these depth: *value focus* is drawn as a third dimension.

Remember that the bottom layer contains all of your sales processes, methodologies, skills, meeting plans, opportunity strategies, etc. where the layers above are how you coach the selling behaviors in the base layer into a consistent operating rhythm. Here, I want to unpack that bottom layer into various components of the selling function. Don't make the mistake of thinking that the selling function happens only in the sales department. Then, for each part of the selling process, I want to talk about the value-oriented coaching that sits in the "above layers" yielding that third dimension.

Value Focus Through the Arc of the Customer Experience

Customers make decisions based only upon what value they perceive. This isn't just final buying decisions, but considerations throughout their buying (and our selling) process. I've said it before: customer-perceived value is the engine powering the entire customer journey. Here's how value focus integrates into the customer and opportunity life cycle:

Demand Creation:

All of today's trendy topics in demand creation rely on communicating customer-recognized value. Persona-based marketing, account-based marketing...they are all predicated on generating customer interest, expressed in customer terms. The best focus on customer outcomes, the foundation of customer value.

Figure 10.2 How value focus tools support Demand Creation

Value networks provide a source of compelling "hooks" for demand generation outreach, content marketing, and the like. This is because value networks specifically link value triggers with specific personas and can be tested and validated via analyzing won/lost deals, especially the value assessments. Relevant content with compelling value messaging drives engagement, a key measure for demand gen.

Success in value-focused demand gen does not merely track clicks and opens. It scores the value drivers *contained in what was clicked or opened*. Crap content generates crap clicks, which can turn into crap leads. When content is about outcomes that result from the selling organization's differentiated offers, those clicks are gold.

Prospecting:

Prospecting is the art of securing an initial appointment. At this early stage, the seller is "selling" a customer an *investment of their time*. Research shows that customers are further into their buying process than ever before granting an appointment, which means they have higher expectations of the value a salesperson should bring. If they don't think a meeting with you is worth their time, your sales process dies before it starts. It's relatively easy for a coach to see pre-call if a seller's reason for meeting shows value for a prospect's time, and easy to coach improvement.

Figure 10.3 How value focus tools support Prospecting

Just as for demand generation stage, a well-thought-out value network provides the basis for compelling justifications for an initial meeting: they offer a clear intersection between a value driver and a specific persona, which should inform prospecting outreach. When those value networks have been validated by similar personas/roles at similar/competing companies, prospecting messages that add value to the target's decision journey become high-probability outreach.

Combining specific persona-targeted value messaging with best prospecting practices, you get a powerful combination. If that prospect has interacted with the demand gen system, and their content interactions are tracked and scored, it becomes easier for a salesperson to develop a solid reason-to-meet...and to deliver valuable insights during that first call.

Business Development:

Business development is a term that means many things to many companies. It can include working with key accounts, with alliance and ecosystem partners, with merger and acquisition partners, or early relationship development in new markets or with previously unaddressed prospects. The whole point of any of these definitions or versions of BizDev is "adding new value," usually "developing unconventional (to that prospect) value." I've done all of these myself, using customer value as the compelling case to get other companies to invest in a shared vision. When we were aligned on customer value, talks were straightforward and pretty smooth. Without customer value, the motivation behind any business relationship began to wane, and strategies between partners diverged.

Regardless of your exact role definition, business development is asking some party in another organization to consider something outside of their normal box. The only way to get somebody comfortable with a new arrangement is to show potential value during every interaction. A common theme in all "versions" of business development is value exploration. Business acumen, a robust understanding of a target's business operations (perhaps courtesy of the business profiling process) helps the business development rep's credibility from that first call, and a robust set of value networks to work from informs high-value dialogue throughout the BD process.

Figure 10.4 How value focus tools support Business Development

In the other direction, business developers are at the forefront of efforts to validate existing value hypotheses and co-create new value with prospects. These need to be carried back through many parts of the selling organization to help formulate offers, design solutions, craft arrangements, and optimize agreements with the highest possible customer value. A common language around value statements is a key focus tool.

Discovery:

In my world (complex B2B consensus selling), and that of most of my clients, discovery is far more than an initial call. Discovery is a multi-person, multi-meeting process that needs to stay on track, guided by customer value. A full set of value networks guides the discovery process, often calling on sellers to engage with unconventional roles/personas/Buying Influences. The insights contained in value networks help sellers establish credibility more quickly by demonstrating immediate value to a prospect

It's never enough to uncover problems and opportunities simply. You don't know how to leverage those things until you know how significant they loom in your prospect's mind; that is, until you develop full value. Sales managers need to coach relentlessly on two things: 1) What is the value of solving problems identified? 2) What is the value of achieving outcomes? If your coaching centers how the customer answers those questions, your sellers will set themselves up for greater success.

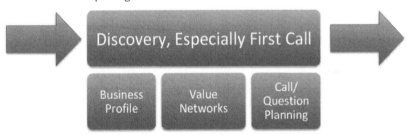

Figure 10.5 How value focus tools support good Discovery

The job of discovery is to learn a prospect's business and find ways to provide valued outcomes. Prospects now expect prepared sellers. Buyers consistently disqualify sellers quickly (disengaging with them) who don't meet expectations. The business acumen tools we've discussed help prevent that failure mode, turning this into a differentiator. Integrating advanced, unconventional insights into a discovery plan positions sellers as valued business advisors and uncovers maximum value.

During a first call or meeting, the relationship between seller and prospect is in its fragile youth. Sellers must 1) build personal credibility, and 2) quickly help the customer determine that engaging with the seller will be worthwhile. This conversation type is too important to "wing it." The value hypothesis must be solid, and the conversation plan must be well-calibrated to the person and situation. Sales leaders can effectively coach how sellers add value to the buying process if there is a meeting plan methodology that clearly demonstrates value focus. Business acumen equips sellers to have meaningful outcome and value-focused *business conversations* rather than selling conversations. These conversations are the difference between salespeople and valued resources.

Channel partners are critical partners in the discovery/value hunting stage. Your best channel partners should be willing to coordinate discovery and have a common language of value-seeking.

The key to having a prospect agree to any action is to have them connect that action with value: this could be taking a step toward achieving a desired outcome, or merely a step toward completing the part of the group buying journey they are connected with.

Opportunity Pursuits:

A complex group buying decision is powered by value. Without value, there is no buying decision. Losing to "no decision" or "status quo" is not because a seller failed to tell or describe value. It's because value failed to form between the right people's ears on the buying side. The difference is often in the failure to have a prospect internalize and/or articulate the value for – and to-- themselves.

Sales methodologies that focus on what each buying influence hopes to achieve on multiple levels are critical for achieving a granular view of each party in a consensus sale. Coach your sellers to not only be able to describe those business and personal outcomes, but to be able to describe the customer-perceived value monetarily. This will help them formulate much more effective selling strategies for each buying decision.

Figure 10.6 How value focus tools support Opportunity Pursuit

Value networks are great frameworks to plan and organize any opportunity pursuit plan. They help develop better, more insightful conversations with every persona involved in a buying decision. Maintaining an active value assessment not only tracks progress but provides an objective measurement of customer value received, which drives your likelihood of successful closing.

Involving more of the right people in the buying decision: Some of the most memorable sales wins I have ever been involved with have been where we found unusual value with some unusual new player…in a role we usually don't sell to. Capitalizing on these opportunities meant scanning the landscape for opportunities to add new, different value propositions into the mix. The only way to reliably replicate those outcomes is to coach your sellers to be sensitive to possible new value. Value networks and business profiles are great tools to help your sellers develop "a nose for value."

Many people in a selling organization may need to be fully briefed in and added to the pursuit, at least temporarily.

Keeping deals on track: As your seller and prospect jointly journey through their respective buying/selling process, prospects are asked to invest progressively in resources, time, and energy. As they engage first in understanding their situation more thoroughly, they then explore and evaluate possible solutions. Good sellers ask prospects to engage in actions that advance their buying process step-by-step. Great sellers will develop – then work -- a jointly developed "plan to go-live" process with the prospect. Elite sellers confirm customer-perceived value at each step in the process. *Helping sales coaches observe* and reinforce this selling behavior is one rewarding part of my practice.

Figure 10.7 How value focus tools support Opportunity Coaching

I once worked in a highly value-focused company who asked one initial coaching question: "what's the value?". When the answer was good, then the coach could be pretty sure that the salesperson had done everything right. When the seller couldn't clearly articulate the value, coaches could dig into the value assessment, the opportunity pursuit plan, or even refer back to any relevant value networks.

A key part of the pursuit process in some businesses is the *product/service demonstration.* These can be opportunities to shine or to lose momentum altogether. The basic maxim of "only demonstrate differentiated value and yada-yada everything else" applies. I recently read a LinkedIn post from Elay Cohen, who described "Twelve Tips for a Sales Demonstration," which are great value-focused advice for keeping demonstrations on-point with value focus[47].

Your Proposal:

It's a big mistake to think your prospect can connect their needs to your solution – even when they've done it before. A major coaching point for proposal prep is to make sure the sales team can clearly recap all of the value gaps they have uncovered, how specific aspects of the proposal address which gaps, which Buying Influences have verified value, and how well the customer as quantified that value.

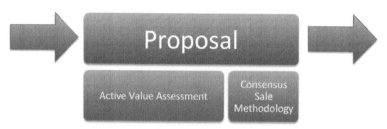

Figure 10.8 How value focus tools support Proposal Development

---

[47] Elay Cohen's LinkedIn post, reproduced here with permission. He doesn't use the exact value focused terms you've been reading in this book, but you'll recognize them:

Here's a checklist of 12 sales demonstration tips:

1) Map your demonstration flow map to business problems and priorities.

2) Create a demonstration flow that answers the why and explains the context.

3) Turn your demonstration flow into a compelling narrative and story with real life examples.

4) Have your demonstration flow talk-track focus on benefits and value versus clicks and features.

5) Validate your demonstration flow with your champion before delivering to all stakeholders.

6) Customize the demonstration flow to make it relevant to the people seeing it.

7) Know your demonstration flow and clicks very well to avoid surprises.

8) Summarize your demonstration flow before you start and at the end too.

9) Frequently pause/stop doing your demonstration flow to get feedback from the meeting participants.

10) Ask open-ended feedback questions doing your demonstration flow like how well are we meeting your expectations.

11) Practice your demonstration flow a few times with your sales team and with your champion if possible.

12) Breathe during your demonstration flow.

An experienced coach can readily help sellers improve offers and presentations. They also can make their own determination of how compelling – and how winnable --an offer is.

Formalized/Artificial Buying Processes:

Far more often than not, (RFIs), RFQs, and RFPs -- or whatever formalized buying process is called in your world -- are flawed processes, overlaying an artificial structure above the real decision they are meant to facilitate. RFx are often used to conceal differentiated value, and to fool a seller into thinking that there is none, driving toward price as the deciding factor.

The main thing to remember is that the RFP process is rarely the decision process. Respect and be responsive to the RFP, but don't let all of the activity in responding to an RFP delude you into thinking you're aligned with the underlying decision process. Keep differences between the two straight, and you will be much more successful.

Where the RFP is often constructed to commoditize competing offers, it is the selling organization's job to differentiate. If the formal process involves a silent period or "cone of silence," the seller's choices are to learn about value before the quiet period, to try to circumvent the quiet period (sometimes dangerous or deal-breaking), or to comply with the embargo and pray. The first is by far the best, of course. Pre-emptively uncovering value using tools like value networks not only positions a selling company to shape requirements but allows your responders to highlight specific value generators in a customized response.

Tom Williams and Tom Saine's The Seller's Challenge, has an entire chapter on RFPs, starting with their four classifications of RFP (Fair, Favored, Fake, and Forced), and going on to a wealth of advice on how to handle RFPs. In addition to recommending this great book[48] yet again, I will add that focusing on the customer value behind the RFP process will help you greatly.

Forecasting:

Forecasting is a major challenge for many sales forces. Predicting the outcome of a sales pursuit is easier when your sales force understands the customer's perceived motivation to buy from you...their perceived incremental value for your offer. Quantify value, and you have the key to understanding a prospect's likely decision.

---

[48] The Seller's Challenge, How Top SellersMaster 10 Deal Killing Obstacles in B2B Sales. Williams, Saine, Strategic Dynamics. ISBN9781948974028

Figure 10.9 Value assessment informs likelihood of purchase and thus forecasting

The same tools that quantify value for pricing confidence provide forecast confidence as well.

Pricing:

Price sensitivity is 100% value sensitivity. I'm fond of telling salespeople that when a customer says, "your price is too high," that I want them to respond as if the customer said, "your value is too low."

The exploration and quantification of value that should occur throughout discovery and pursuit should form a solid basis for pricing discussions. Coaching sellers to validate and monetize customer value makes price negotiations much more productive and win-win.

Figure 10.10 How value focus tools support price setting and discounting strategy

The value analysis worksheet collects all of the findings from value mining and discovery throughout an opportunity pursuit. During price-setting and negotiation, the value analysis on that worksheet provides objective data as the basis.

Territory Management:

Territory management is a prioritization and time management exercise, not a customer-facing activity per se. Because a salesperson's most precious resource is time, salespeople faced with large account portfolios find that tools to focus time investment are mission-critical.

Extensive tools are available for target/prospect scoring and opportunity scoring. Some are simple scoring tools; others are sophisticated artificial intelligence (OK, probably just big data analytics with an optimistic marketing spin). Any prospect scoring system is an attempt to understand fit. Fit is (or should be) defined as the value of outcomes that the customer is likely to realize from a seller's offer. Value-based predictive analysis should be a significant part of a scoring system used for time and territory management. Value networks and historical value analyses from similar customers can form the underpinning of such analytic tools, making them more robust.

Channel Management:

In addition to the customer realizing value from your offer, any indirect channel partners used to get your offer into their hands should realize value from working with you (margins, key products for one of their markets, etc.) – in exchange for providing value (such as customer access, breaking bulk, performing key sales functions, etc.) to your firm. They should also add value to the customer experience.

Understanding potential value exchange between channel partners informs many decisions, including choosing and/or recruiting the right partners.

When working with partners, it's always important to know who adds what value. We'll talk about it later, but remember that partners can add value: relationships you don't have, geographic coverage, knowing key buying influences you don't, providing wraparound value that you can't. These value exchanges help guide:

- Choosing/recruiting partners
- Capability mapping, the process of making sure you and your partners complement each other.
- Aligning/avoiding conflict
- Role allocation
- Motivating your partner

Between-sale/post-sale execution (installation, implementation, client/customer success, and more):

In any business where repeat sales are an integral part of the business model, "post-sale" programs would be more accurately called *between sale* care. As your company starts delivering on a won order, having everyone on the implementation team aware of what all players/personas in the buying organization were expecting to achieve helps implementation experts meet and exceed customer expectations, anticipate problems, and deepen customer relationships.

In addition to technical statements of work, specs, and agreements, I advise clients to incorporate persona-specific expectations into handoff (from sales to execution) packages. Value expectations add a critical depth of customer understanding that statements of work, product specifications, deliverables, and service level agreements just don't capture.

Figure 10.11 Closing loops between sales using value focus tools.

Radical value focus means capitalizing on customer relationships in deep-reaching ways. Implementation/delivery associates have a view into – and trusting relationships with -- parts of the customer organization that few other roles can access. Giving them the same tools to uncover, understand, and describe value – both to the customer and back into the selling organization – re-establishes the customer intimacy that organizations lost when they split their customer interface into slivers.

There is an increasing awareness that the full arc of the customer experience needs to be a series of well-aligned functions and operations. This awareness has spawned the term Customer Experience, or CX, as the cool kids call it. Post-sale touchpoints like technical support, customer support, billing inquiries & adjustments, etc. are all potential areas in which to lose customer...or, build insurmountable customer loyalty barriers against competition.

What is less acknowledged is that these increasingly key roles are "observation posts," each of which has an intimate view of the customer experience seldom witnessed by other sellers. Supplying the training and tools for people at every customer touchpoint gives the organization a more complete and holistic view of customer-perceived value. These tools need to be as "incidental" as possible. That is, present as little additional work as possible. Some of this can be met with sophisticated tools like advanced analytics and voice analytics (extracting information directly from phone conversations with machines doing the transcription and analytics), but tools as simple as the value network do a great job as well when combined with the appropriate training.

Current thought in modern CX (customer experience) management is roughly as follows:

- **"Good" CX:** make sure no customer-facing people do any harm to the relationship.

- **"High-level" CX:** empowering people to deliver a great experience. I agree, but I want to add an additional level:

- **"Radical" CX:** every customer-facing person coached to understand the value dynamic they are building, extract value insights from customer interactions, and to incorporate value insights into the corporation (aggregated value networks).

Every customer-facing role should understand value language, value networks, where they impact customer outcomes, and how to uncover and develop new value gaps.

Relationship Management:

Any company in the business of generating repeat business has one or more of these roles: key account managers, account managers, channel managers, or sales generalists with existing account management duties. All are charged with making customer relationships stronger. The driving force of relationship management is perceived customer value.

Columbia University's Noel Capon wrote the gold-standard manual on key account management, and some methodologies operationalize much of Capon's work, filling key execution gaps. The central goal is evolving from a series of transactions with a big customer to aggregating the outcomes of those transactions into a mutually beneficial relationship.

Figure 10.12 How value focus tools support Relationship Management

Programs to deepen relationships should pass through a two-part screening exercise: articulate differentiation to a customer, and have the customer articulate sufficient value of the outcome produced. This is true for inexpensive support programs like business tracking all the way to major initiatives like strategic acquisitions to support a future customer need (yes, I've seen it done).

Similarly, for anyone working even partly in an account management role, business acumen is key. It helps them focus on how their firm's offer adds value to a customer's business. Conversations around this value are the lever that moves relationships.

As stated earlier, execution professionals and client success professionals have unique access to a customer's company. Even if they aren't given an expectation for new sales, they should be incentivized and equipped to uncover value gaps and to engage colleagues appropriately.

I like to think of it this way:

Empowering your people is good.

Empowering well-informed and insight-laden people is great.

Coaching all your people to gather value insights is elite.

We've gone through many of the important parts of the customer journey, describing how a shift to value focus changes their character in important, fundamental ways – but without significantly increasing their complexity or difficulty.

The return on this investment in customer value focus: more sales, and more profitable sales, higher customer preference.

Key Take-Aways

Corporate Leaders: Even if you don't reorganize your company like Mike Houlihan and Bonnie Harvey organized Barefoot Wines into two departments, sales and sales support, I hope you've come around to the basic idea. Customer value is the source of all demand, and everyone in our company had better be aligned to value. I understand the motivation to form specialist functions of different groups who interact with your customers, but you need to balance expertise against the risks associated with splintering your customer interface into too many uncoordinated groups. Regardless of the organizational structures you implement to manage that risk, it's imperative that all groups adopt a universal language of customer value, and that the arc of the customer experience is value-focused.

Sales Leaders: Without getting into the politics of chief revenue officer, chief customer officer, or VP of Sales, there is no doubt that you need to lead the charge for a unified, coordinated approach among all customer-facing roles. The language of value focus can be a common binder among many specialist departments and help all add value to one another. I hope that the recitation of value focus at many points along the selling/customer experience journey helped you envision what value focus will look like in any selling organization, and what the high points of value coaching should feel like.

Sales Enablement Leaders: This book introduces tools (business profiles, value networks, value calculators) used throughout the sellers' (and buyers') journey. This chapter should provide some depth of view into how these tools enrich each part of the selling arc. Envisioning the improved selling outcomes from adopting them should be pretty straightforward.

I look forward to your doing a value analysis for adopting them into your selling operation. Teaching, tracking, and coaching to value is easy and intuitive for sellers. If you introduce these tools alongside your "new" profit-oriented sales incentive program, your people should be eager and willing to adopt them.

Sales Operations Leaders: This chapter was very seller-focused, with a lot of emphasis on sales roles. I laid out a roadmap for which of the tools this book introduces (business profiles, value networks, value calculators) are used throughout the sales journey. I hope you find this helpful. I've also given some guidance for when/how different an opportunity management sales methodology tool integrates into a value-focused sales system. I did not mention call planning and conversational skills since those should be intertwined into everything your sellers do with customers. They're so essential and so universal that I didn't call them out.

Sellers: Whichever specific customer-facing role you perform, I wanted to break the sales process down into stages, and discuss how value focus tools impact each part. I hope this chapter provided some specific guidelines for you at each part of the journey of optimizing customer value from lead gen to fulfillment.

Marketing Professionals: I'll be talking to you directly at the beginning of the next chapter, but I wanted you to see the sales process in detail, and then describe how value focus enriches each part. Marketing is a critical resource for making that enrichment happen.

Product/Service Professionals: I'll be talking to you directly inf the next chapter as well. Like marketing, I wanted you to see the sales process in detail, and then describe how value focus enriches each part.

Chapter
ELEVEN

A Day in the Life: What's Different About a Radically Value Focused Organization?

A value-focused organization is different from its bland "for-profit" and its frustrating "for process" counterparts. Value focus is more actionable than "customer-focused culture" in that people have a clear language and thought process for prioritizing precisely what about the customer needs to be focused on. I want to walk you through a value-focused organization from the customer in. While the last chapter was sales and seller focused, this chapter works inward from the customer: initially from sellers (everyone who touches the customer) to marketing.

Ending Sales / Marketing Turf Wars: Let Customer Value Win

Let's face it: friction between Sales and Marketing functions has existed since {insert favorite dinosaur or Old Testament reference here}. The problem isn't different goals; each has the same goal but different vantage points. I've spent chunks of my career in each function and have seen both effectiveness and dysfunction from each perspective.

Marketing is a discipline of identifying groups of people with commonalities and communication to these groups (usually) in a one-to-many format. It follows that lead generation is often viewed as a bulk process with indistinguishable units (contacts/leads) making up a homogeneous stream. By contrast, the essence of Sales lies in individualized communication to every single customer, tailored to specific individuals within that customer. These divergent viewpoints are the source of most of the friction. The notion of a "value message," a single statement of value that one can whip out and smack every customer in the face with, is indicative of these different perspectives. I like the idea of a repeatable value *proposition*; I just think propositions are useless until a customer has engaged with them, envisioned their outcomes, begun telling themselves a personal adoption story, and validated (at least some aspect of) the blurb...in order to get a real complex sales conversation started.

> *Apologies to those in simple selling situations where the cost of a sales conversation isn't worth the additional value premium achievable...and in which you can make lots of sales en masse by simply stating your value proposition. Good on you. I know that is a big part of the world, just not the part I work in.*

How can value focus help refocus these two essential functions on a common mission? When marketing manages and curates the collection of value insights., they have the resources to use those insights meaningfully.

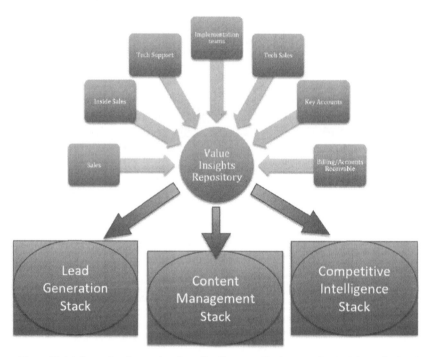

Figure 11.1 Information flows, showing all sellers contributing to value insights, which inform a variety of marketing functions

There are three primary interfaces or interaction points between Sales and Marketing. Let's look at each:

1: Competitive Analysis

When either Sales or Marketing performs competitive analysis in isolation, the result can disappoint. A best practice is to have Marketing curate a common knowledge base that combines Marketing's global "big picture" analysis with more anecdotal on-the-ground competitive reports from actual Sales interactions and opportunity pursuits.

When Sales has a robust value selling methodology in place, actual value analysis worksheets provide customer-validated insights on differentiation. Value worksheets identify specific competitors and recap actual customer value comparisons. This kind of detail is never available to traditional marketing CI (competitive analysis) and is critical information for sellers. Marketing should have access to value analysis worksheets in a well-run value-focused organization.

Having ready access to a library of value assessment sheets is a powerful tool, giving sales the ability to more effectively and efficiently differentiate in the future. Consistently used, seller value discipline provides unrelenting alertness for changes in the differentiation landscape; as competitors change, value-focused companies know about it, understand the nature and severity of any changes, and are more able to adapt quickly.

2: Leads provided by Marketing to Sales

Lead quality can be a significant bone of contention: Sales can seldom afford the time to find good leads buried within a stack of bad ones. Of course, Marketing needs deals won from the lead stack to show ROI for its efforts. Lead quality – measured as "acceptable to Sales" – is the key. In this case, the tie goes to customer value. Sales, whose most limited resource is time, can find time to work on leads containing a clear line-of-sight to customer value. Marketing needs to adjust their KPIs to weigh lead quality more heavily than lead quantity, which means scoring leads against customer outcomes and value they've indicated an interest in.

Best marketing practice is to:

1. Develop value-focused lead pre-qualification, scoring systems and screening to an Ideal Customer Profile

2. Track the value proposition that drove clicks and opens, not just the number of clicks and opens

Sophisticated data analytics to operationalize the lead pre-qualification process is coming into its own, but performing analytics using the right criteria is essential.

Lead quality improves dramatically when scored against value networks and value assessment worksheets of previously won opportunities. These inform scoring and segmenting, emphasizing the most leverageable value gaps.

3: Selling Support tools provided by Marketing to Sales

This area has seen a proliferation of technology tools that give marketing visibility into which assets are most effective, at what stage in the customer's buying cycle, and by what personas. These tools guide creative Marketers toward producing **value- and outcome-focused content** and marketing assets.

Value networks and value analysis worksheets for won (and lost) opportunities give both Sales and Marketing better insight into buying processes. Assets which focus on the buying process "sticking points" for specific personas should be a point of emphasis. Business profiles, value networks, and the value assessments that they spawn sharpen messaging dramatically. Using them, marketers can gain a direct view of the impact of each differentiator and a deeper understanding of the value dynamic at a customer. Assets become outcome-oriented, powerful story-telling pieces.

High-Level Coordination Between Sales and Marketing: ABM

Account based marketing (or ABM) is a great development in marketing practice. From my work in Sales, though, I think of the basic approach as an extension of consensus selling strategies used for decades by sales organizations: a customized, persona-specific approach to every opportunity. I love that the Marketing discipline is harnessing powerful technologies, applying their creativity, efficiency, and talent into an individually personalized approach that was previously the exclusive domain of sales. I hope that anyone thinking of embarking on an ABM initiative will realize that it can only be effective as a tightly coordinated multidisciplinary effort between sales and marketing.

A good introductory article in Direct Marketing News[49]: describes ABM as "a strategic approach to integrated, branded communications to customers and prospects that treats an individual account as its own highly specialized market opportunity." Another definition is similar: "a strategic approach to business marketing [50] in which an organization considers and communicates with individual prospect or customer accounts as markets of one. Account-based marketing is typically employed in enterprise-level sales organizations".

---

[49] http://www.dmnews.com/dataanalytics/account-based-marketing-how-it-can-help-your-company-improve-demand-awareness-and-profitability/article/98038/

[50] https://en.wikipedia.org/wiki/Business_marketing

As opposed to traditional "lead-based" marketing, an account-based approach spends a lot of up-front resources in defining an ideal customer profile, targeting high-probability accounts, and then – like a consensus selling practitioner has always done – do the work of penetrating personas within that account and facilitating multi-person buying decisions. Marketing digs for not just contact information but backgrounds, provides decision-specific content targeting specific personas, and builds on success by repeating the process for cross- and upsell opportunities.

The kind of micro-targeting that ABM demands has only become technologically feasible in the last decade or so – cost-effective for only part of that time. The last few years have seen a tremendous maturing of the field and establishment of best practices. Once, human interaction was the only/best source of actionable account-specific information, but no more. Modern tools, mastered by Marketers, help companies perform ultra-targeted communication to more influencers at more companies than sales can cost-effectively identify and address. The mass-efficiency of a Marketing campaign combined with individualization formerly requiring sales is a potent tool.

The tools and common language presented in this book take today's ABM to a high-impact, highly targeted tool. Value-driven target identification, personalized message optimization, and customer journey mapping supported by value networks all bring deep customer insight to ABM.

When ABM is done right:

1. ABM guides, facilitates, and accelerates a customer journey.

2. Responds adaptively to make each journey as interactive as possible.

3. Seamlessly engages live people who will respond appropriately and proactively.

4. Tracks progress through a journey and analyzes best next steps.

5. Dovetails with sales, helping them be more prepared to conduct conversations without missing a beat.

For most business-to-business selling, ABM can make for significant efficiency gains. ...and more importantly: serious effectiveness gains.

Value focus can inform and enrich the best marketing practices. Importantly, a common language of customer-perceived value can provide a framework for alignment between these two functions.

Value-Driven Best Practices in Product Management

As a former product manager, I have a strong point of view on what the role should and shouldn't be. I fully understand that the job description of "Product

Manager" at a consumer-packaged-goods company is unrecognizable from the same title at a technology company. Let's side-step job description/title differences and talk about how value focus enriches any product management role (even if it's divided into several to many titles in your particular company).

Product Training for Sellers: all Customer-Facing Roles

Every Sales professional (and some other seller roles) is familiar with a common first order of business: getting trained upon the products and services of their organization.

I've gone through many of these, and as a product manager, created and delivered product training. I've seen good, bad, and everything in between. Let's focus on some best practices here.

There are several areas that great product training needs to cover:

The Basics

Yes, every product must include the basic product features, standards, specs... "speeds and feeds" [51] information. While compulsory, this is the least compelling from a differentiation/value point of view. This means while it's interesting to the product people and a few technically oriented personas, it's the least relevant to top-performing sellers.

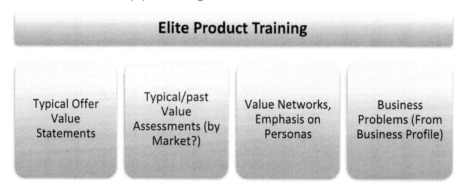

Figure 11.2 How value focus tools inform Elite Product Training

Elite Product Training is Value Focused and includes a deep dive into how the product or services find value in your customer base.

---

[51] Trivia: An industrial drill press in a metal machine shop has settings for drill RPM (speed), and one for how many thousandths of an inch the drill is fed into the work per revolution (feed). Setting the speed and feeds wrong can ruin parts. The phrase now means generally "in-the-weeds/operator level technical detail".

Common Differentiators

All product training programs should emphasize differentiated product/service advantages with clearly articulated (outcome-focused) relevance to one or more Personas. Differentiators should be clearly connected to customer outcomes. Pooled-experience-derived value networks (which can be applied to multiple prospective customers, say, in an industry) are a powerful tool for product training – they help salespeople connect differentiators to personas more firmly and memorably.

When value networks are combined with a complex/consensus selling methodology (selling into a group buying decision), sellers are equipped with tools to secure and conduct meetings with those contacts, as well as how to formulate and execute a strategy around that group buying decision. Since value drives the customer journey, building sales strategies and meeting plans built upon value development are more powerful. Providing clear linkages between product/service differentiators and a selling strategy makes for very powerful product training.

A powerful value communication tool is the "Offer Value Statement," sometimes called the "Product Concept Statement." It describes the offer's (product or service) unique value-producing characteristic or combination of characteristics in objectively measurable feature terms. When a product group can boil their uniqueness down into a single sentence, sales has a clear path to finding and developing value in the mind of a customer.

> An example Value Statement from my past goes something like: "The only commercial mortgage having both bank-like prepay penalties *and* a 25 year fully amortizing term". It turns out that you can build a pretty large, pretty profitable company on that value statement.

Common Applications/Use Cases

When a product is sold into multiple industries, product training should familiarize sellers with common applications and/or use cases. How do customers use the product/service? What problems or issues does it solve for them? What outcomes does it help them achieve? Answering these questions during product training reinforces the value of your product, and illustrating outcomes is much more important than basic speeds and feeds.

A business profiling exercise should help with detailing where to look for value. Value networks track how and where key outcomes are achieved. If your product or service helps make the customer more profitable or more competitive, product training should carefully detail the mechanics of that outcome and how to discuss it/with whom. When the product/service solves some hidden problem(s), the profile should help identify it – again, with persona-based sales guidance.

Product training on applications should also include common terminology and language for target markets and customers to help salespeople quickly build credibility with prospects.

Competition...Specifically, Value-centered Competitive Analysis

Basic product training usually gives a nod to major competitors. Competent product training covers comparisons/differences from a specs/performance standpoint. Great product training uses past value analysis worksheets to share how past customers have valued differentiators for major customer types. This helps quantify which differentiators deliver how much value.

Persona-based differentiation points are another best practice; they provide granular competitive information that salespeople find highly actionable. Value networks are a great way to develop persona-based differentiation hypotheses.

Completed Value Analysis worksheets are easy to review and validate in after-action/won-deal reviews. They should be curated somewhere: in sales, marketing or product owners, or sales operations. They provide highly actionable information for sellers in the form of how specific competitors compare in actual sales situations.

Good product training can articulate not just differentials in features and capabilities, but how those advantages turn into outcomes. Great product training equips sellers to understand customer outcomes – in financial terms. A tiny component that reduces the downtime in a major industrial customer's process can have value thousands of times its price. Sellers need to know how to walk through that math with a customer...or be susceptible to unwarranted discounting pressure.

Offer Value Statements/Product Concept statements sharpen customer conversations around compelling, differentiated value in use. They can distill competitive discussions into the essential elements.

Common Buying Personas/Buying Influences

While I firmly believe that every customer makes every buying decision differently every time, there are almost always some recurring themes, plus a few common variants to buying decisions. The more product training prepares sellers on what to expect, the better. A best practice in product training is to overview the common personas encountered in a typical sale. For each major market segment, sellers should leave product training knowing:

- Typical buying ecosystems: personas, and role in the decision.
- Common buyer journey overviews

- High-leverage personas: those who typically have high value-affinity for the product's unique advantages.

- Mapping advantages to common personas.

- Value analysis worksheets help sellers see the relative value contribution of differentiators. This informs the priority of different personas in an opportunity pursuit.

An especially important detail: how and when to expand the buying ecosystem (engage with additional personas) to capitalize on additional value creation: looking for unconventional value. Creative additions to the buying ecosystem which creative sellers have uncovered, previously discovered unique value propositions, are all high-level additions.

Selling Resources

In some companies with widely varied products, there can be different selling playbooks in place. If you own a product P&L, you are ultimately responsible for the quality, availability, and especially applicability of selling resources and playbooks. I discussed many of the issues you face under the marketing function above. Depending upon your relationship with…and access to marketing as a resource, responsibilities for those items might move into the product realm. Either way, the success of your product depends on the quality of selling resources no matter who has the responsibility for producing them.

This includes selling resource libraries and policies. Where are value networks and do sellers know how to use them? Where are the brochures, presentations, videos, and white papers kept, and how do they map to specific portions of buying journeys? A best practice is to capture common "sticking points" in typical buyer journeys and (make sure marketing?) develop(s) content which helps salespeople and customers navigate those sticking points more effectively. Making it easy for sellers to do this is a hallmark of world-class product training.

Value Focus in Product Design and Development

Since customers buy outcomes, not our products and services, product groups need a clear connection between what the selling organization sells and what the customer buys.

The price customers pay for those outcomes is commensurate with how they value *all* outcomes (direct and ancillary, business and personal) achieved. If the product group is to maximize profitability, they need to understand outcomes to price insightfully.

As product owners and developers plan and execute new product and service deliverables, they need more than the voice of the customer: what the customer knows to ask for. They need to know the *mind of the customer:* all of their business challenges, where value resides, and how outcomes are achieved. Value networks and business profiles help product teams understand how customer outcomes are produced. Business profiles help product teams develop creative high-value solutions to critical customer problems. Using these tools enables a common language that helps the entire company operationalize a culture of continuous value improvement.

Advanced Product Development Tools

Agile development is a product development paradigm characterized by incremental stepwise development. Value focus is not a replacement or a competitor, but the big picture insight and overall direction informing a methodology like Agile.

The "Agile Manifesto" stresses customer collaboration, a "what" I strongly support; collaboration focused on customer outcomes, and customer value becomes the "how" and sharpens any customer actions, prioritizing developments, and sometimes allowing developers to innovate in ways that customers didn't know how to articulate. Agile practitioners should be trained on conducting customer value conversations so that they can pack the most customer value into each sprint (product version/release, for the non-Agile conversant). Customers can ask for a lot of things. Talking them through the value of their requests helps both sides get comfortable that each next step is packed with the highest value.

Collaboration isn't just talking with customers, or just asking. It's about understanding and anticipating. It's about looking beyond customer requests and understanding customer outcomes and customer value. Business profiles provide a great framework/starting point for collaborative discussions with customers. Value networks help developers think more holistically. Using the same tools that sellers and marketing use facilitates common language, and also facilitates any marketing or sales messaging that follows the development, especially to follow-on customers.

The tools of value focus enrich methodologies like Agile, Scrum, and Kanban. They provide a true north for the team: customer perceived value. The tools of value acumen bring better insight into the development world in an easy-to-consume form.

Other tools use small, iterative thinking not in product development, but in business plan//business model/business strategy development and risk mitigation. I use one, called the Real-Win-Worth[52] screening tool, with new products clients, but that's another book.

Value networks add a third dimension, customer outcomes, to two-dimensional new product requirements documents. Employees in customer-interacting roles –sellers -- can carry invaluable insights to the product role when they communicate customer-experienced value. This improves customer value for new products, growing sales of existing products, or finding new applications for existing products.

When everyone in your company understands the language of customer-perceived value, new products are more impactful to customers, which helps them be more successful. It's easy to convey how little product changes can yield significant competitive advantages (or the opposite).

Value Drives Your Intellectual Property Strategy

Value is derived from differentiation. Some kinds of differentiation can be protected with patents. Patents don't exist to allow the inventor to do something, but to prevent others from doing something. When differentiation is patented, it can be protected until the patent expires, or someone leapfrogs the patent.

Good patentable inventions may be inventions that let you increase the average selling price, decrease per-unit cost, and/or capture sales for differentiation features (compared to the best-unpatented alternative). The patent creates value for your company if it *keeps competitors from following*. Here are some examples:

- Protecting margins or sales volumes for existing products, new products, line extension products, or product redeployments into new markets. For instance, if your company has a product that creates a new market, and a patent can exclude all competitors from that market, then patents are especially valuable.

- Next-generation products in established markets.

- Product differentiators that can raise market share or command a higher price.

Many, many patents are directed to cost reductions:

- Manufacturing cost advantages that can be used to improve margins or reduce sale price—typically manufacturing machines or methods, test machines or methods, etc.

---

[52] https://hbr.org/2007/12/is-it-real-can-we-win-is-it-worth-doing-managing-risk-and-reward-in-an-innovation-portfolio

- Business methods, especially those that are core to the business model.

A patent may be valuable to increase your client's sales:

- Blocking patents that raise rivals' costs, even if you are not practicing the invention.

- Patents that cover the next-best way of solving a problem, to protect the competitive flank of your company's actual products. Such patents may arise out of research and development (R&D) projects that were rejected, prototypes that were replaced by more-promising approaches, or for retired products.

- Patents can provide marketing or advertising gloss, the customer's perception of value

There are a few ways that a patent can generate a return that are not directly related to the patented product:

- A patent may give bargaining leverage with a key supplier or strategic partner.

- If competitors know of your patents, they may choose to stay out of specific markets. This is especially likely in "thin margin" industries.

A Patent May Provide Useful Leverage with Strategic Partners

Patents can be used in negotiating relationships with strategic partners. Here's an example.

Company A, the largest company in its industry, owned an invention that was worth perhaps $100 million per year. However, they didn't have the infrastructure for retail delivery. Company A formed a strategic partnership with its occasional vertical partner Company B, also the largest in its industry. Company B had that infrastructure, and together they formed a joint venture to market the invention. Company A had the business relationships needed to make the invention work, and because this was a service business, Company A's customer list and partnership relationships were the single most crucial asset contributed to the joint venture. The joint venture was to run two years.

But Company B had patents on the infrastructure. Company A recognized that Company B's patent rights would be sufficient to exclude Company A from the business after the joint venture ended. Thus, Company A spent two years building a business, gained some profits during the two years, but then agreed to walk away and hand the business—and the client relationships—over to Company B.

Value Focus Throughout Your Organization

A culture of continuous value improvement touches every part of the enterprise, and every part of the enterprise should have a direct line between their function and customer value delivered and should be incentivized to innovate customer value.

Legal departments deserve to be called out in particular, even though they occupy a single point along the customer experience arc. Legal can establish a point of "pride" in being challenging to work with – although I can happily claim to work with some who took pride in their customer focus. In many companies, being hard to do business with is a legal group "persona," which conflicts with the company's brand promise. In fairness, those in legal silos are seldom given insight into their counter-party's expected outcomes and value expectations. A wiser balance between risk mitigation and making progress on business arrangements is sometimes in order. When legal groups are given value insights, expect better alignment to company operations.

Mergers & Acquisitions based on "financial synergies" often disappoint. If management can clearly identify new value networks yielded by a business combination, and at least preliminarily verify customer value in a new set of outcomes, a business combination can withstand the inevitable operational challenges and unexpected snags. When there is a clear vision of how the combined companies will deliver value, newly combined teams have a much clearer charter than most acquisitions I experienced early in my career.

Purchasing is not "my tribe" as a lifelong seller, but I've worked with the role a lot. While their charter is to secure the best value, that often turns out to be actualized as the best possible price and delivery outcome. Formalized purchasing processes often gloss over value received by the organization by not providing purchasing people with the business acumen to judge outcomes fairly. Applying my experience in broadening buying decisions to maximize customer value, it's essential to help procurement understand the broader scope of value for their company, to recognize when their process is obscuring value received, and build in incentives to focus on value vs. price.

Manufacturing: I've worked with a company that has incorporated value discipline all the way to the factory floor – a pretty radical step. They can't get a production operator to invest even ten minutes on a prototype unless a "priceable" value premium over the competitive alternative can be demonstrated. It was maddening at times to be sure, but weaving customer-centric valuation and pricing into the corporate culture has had industry-leading, long-term (over 50 years at this company) profitability results.

Channel Partners. The exchange of value (achieving desirable outcomes) is at the very core of choosing the right channel arrangements, motivating channel partners, reducing channel conflict; in short, every element of the channel strategy. Channel partners offload burdens (typically selling, breaking bulk, customer service, etc.) from their principals in exchange for margin dollars and support programs.

<u>Human Resources</u>: Building a culture of continuous value improvement is a company-wide endeavor. In my experience, two things are true: 1) HR is a key player, 2) HR is often eager to make initiatives like this a success. I'll talk a bit about change management later. Do yourself a favor: if you are trying to implement a value-focused culture, engage HR early and effectively...in this, or any "deep culture change" project. How they recruit, how they help you communicate, staff, and train can be a major success factor.

<u>Board of Directors</u>: As I quoted earlier, McKinsey found that only 22% of board members could clearly articulate the value their company provided[53]. This needs to improve. Value focus needs to extend to the boardroom, or the company's leaders can't align with their customers.

A disciplined, proactive approach to value focus works well when focused on a sales organization, better when confined to sales and marketing, and best when it permeates the entire enterprise. Ultimately, value focus can be executed with several feedback loops. We'll talk about this future of value focus in the final chapter.

Key Take-Aways

Corporate Leaders: Organizing around the principle of Customer-perceived value is a simple concept but involves a host of small changes. This chapter described a lot of "what value focus looks like" all around your company.

Sales Leaders: This chapter was about what needs to change in every group in your company...except yours. Be sensitive to what needs to change and how challenging all of that is while insisting on what value focus requires of everyone in your company. You may need to bring a lot of people along with this change...people you don't have positional authority over. That will be a real test of your salesmanship and leadership.

Sales Enablement and Operations Leaders: This chapter has been about how functions outside of yours implement a value-focused culture. Sales Enablement especially needs to understand these cross-organizational dynamics and be ready to help those struggling to implement. You can be the internal company center of excellence for understanding how different organizations throughout your company use the language and tools of value-focused organizations.

---

[53] Improving Corporate Governance. McKinsey Global Survey Results. 2013. McKinsey also did this study in 2012, with similar, but not identical results

Sellers: This may have been an interesting chapter for you. While everything in it affected you, and a lot of these functional changes will impact you positively, they aren't in your department. Look at this chapter as an exercise in business acumen. As we talk about how value reaches tentacles across organizations, it parallels how value focus will reach across yours. Here's an example of how your sale can have impacts in many unexpected places.

Marketing Professionals: It might be that marketing is the host for value networks and/or value assessment worksheets. How you execute your role as "the value library" for the entire company will shape the success of the shift to value focus.

Product/Service Professionals: You may be interacting with some new people within your company as you evangelize value focus throughout your organization. This chapter may shine some new light on who those people might be and what they will need to enact value focus within their roles.

Chapter
TWELVE

How Radical Value Focus Changes Your Customer Relationships

What Happens Between a Value Focused Enterprise and Its Customers

A company which focuses on customer value:

- Offers higher, deeper, more mutually understood value. This drives higher customer satisfaction *and* better pricing.

- Is engaged with customers more widely. More customer-facing roles are integrally involved, and more of their customer-side counterparts feel well-served and value both the offer and their relationships with the selling company's representatives.

- Has a deeper understanding of what customers truly value and why. Leaders can make better resource allocation decisions

We've discussed a disciplined approach to value, describing it as a company-wide culture rather than merely a sales skill. I've made the case that value-focused companies are different than others, especially those who are shareholder value-focused, or quarterly results-focused.

Customer value-focused companies are radically different than "customer-focused" companies. I talk to executives who know instinctively that customer focus makes sense, but don't know how to operationalize the ideal. I wrote this book to address that gap. I grow businesses for a living and have no use for principles without actionable tools.

How the Value Focus Tools Work Together

I've described several tools to collect, discover, curate, and communicate value insights: Value Networks, Business Profiles, Value Assessments, and Offer Value

Statements. They are all simple to understand and use, and easy to use collaboratively (the best practice).

- Business Profiles are background documents to gain insight into a customer's world quickly and focus attention on where value can be uncovered. There can be surprising differences between companies in the same industry.

- Offer value statements describe the primary differentiation of a product/service. If this is at the gross market level, the value statement informs product development, improvement, and marketing. They make a good summary of value at the opportunity level but are no substitute for a full value assessment.

- Value networks can be general, industry-directed, or customer-specific. They collect persona-specific value hypotheses in a graphic format that informs and guides a pursuit.

- Value Assessments are customer- and pursuit-specific. They inform the pursuit, pricing, and forecasting. They can be useful as guides for similar (similar customer, similar market) pursuits as well.

Any customer-facing person attuned to customer value can contribute/add to either a value network or value assessment for a product. Team selling is similar: everyone working with the same customer should collaboratively work on a single assessment and/or network. As an opportunity pursuit progresses, the assessment matures and is linked with the opportunity pursuit strategy – but isn't a substitute for the pursuit methodology.

Value assessments and networks distill customer value for use by Marketing, Product, Business Development, …every other function in the selling company.

Value Focus in All Customer-Facing Roles

All value is in the mind of the customer, yet since sales carry only part of the customer experience responsibility, sales should not operate on an island without all customer-facing colleagues. That said, sales is almost always the function charged with securing a profitable sale. While your company may differ from this model (I'm happy to help you apply the tools optimally to your unique situation), let's discuss the common situation where many customer-facing organizations *could gather* customer value insights, but where the primary company interface to customer commitment is sales. Information should be collected from all contact points. With these insights, a sales organization is better equipped, compensated, and empowered to help customers discover value, then describe it in currency-denominated detail.

Any sales methodology that engages a prospective customer in detail, and uncovers new value gaps (call them needs, wants, fears, pain points, gaps, opportunities, aspirations, etc.) is a foundational starting point. Sales methodologies embody some basic building blocks: having insightful customer interactions and developing/uncovering value gaps.

Whatever methodology you choose as your foundation, make sure that it focuses on aligning sellers with the customer buying process, and has all of the post-training-event behavior reinforcement and sustainment tools that your corporate culture needs to accomplish long-term adoption. In other words: don't buy just training – invest in a comprehensive plan to establish a new operating cadence – this may involve a corporate culture shift and all of the change management tools that go with that. Some external training companies are better at helping clients build the kind of sustainment and adoption plans that ensure long-term success. Whether you are building your own or buying, make sure that you have a clear idea of how you will be ensuring behavior change at the individual level.

When those foundational tools are combined with tools that:

- Give every customer-facing person the business acumen to quickly explore the value that competitors don't and the ability to discuss value gaps with customers collaboratively. Every team must contribute to the search for value. A seller becomes a trusted advisor when they can give a meaningful perspective to a buyer, and the higher a seller tries to reach within a target company, the broader and more strategic that perspective needs to be. A seller who understands everything about how their offer affects the department that buys and uses it isn't all that valuable to many adjacent departments, or the Vice President they all report to.

- Give customer-facing teams the tools to develop full value around each differentiator systematically. This way, those differentiators achieve maximum value and maximum leverage in the customer's buying decision.

- Engage the customer at a deep level, thoroughly internalizing value by monetizing it. This way, that value has maximum immediacy and impact through the customer decision process.

When such tools are simple to understand, adopt, and integrate into the operating rhythm, you get maximum impact with minimum wasted motion.

To re-emphasize: the more of a business generalist each seller is, the more impact they can find for your product/service. Selling methodologies applied over a foundation of business acumen become keys to achieving greater credibility, access to higher decision levels, and delivering higher customer preference at higher price premiums.

Another key point to recap: A selling organization populated with people capable of facilitating a customer process of envisioning outcomes associated with a value driver is a competitive advantage. This capability differentiates normal sales organizations from extraordinary—radically value focused ones. Your people should consistently facilitate a customer envisioning process, which builds a bridge between outcome, value, and purchase. This is a critical step in preventing "no-decisions," those cases where the customer likes your solution but isn't yet motivated to move ahead with a purchase decision.

While many selling methodologies help facilitate an effective customer journey through the "decision to buy," few methodologies go the last critical step that joins value drivers in a direct line to price (I can show you one). Without this critical connection, price discussions are guided by:

1. Some tactic/counter-tactic negotiation method. Sellers are trained to counter the common ploys used by (especially purchasing) buying influences. These tactics become less effective with top-level and economic buying influences. More critically, customer value becomes simply a bystander to combat; ongoing relationships between the parties are collateral damage, and final price is a damaged trophy.

2. Treating price as just another feature to be traded off. At its best, this approach empowers sellers to reduce price – or offer to do so -- in exchange for removing some attributes of the product. More commonly, though, sales places price on equal footing with any other removable feature of their offer, and price is dropped until customer resistance drops to a level matching increasing company financial resistance.

3. An interest-based negotiation method, where underlying interests are explored for out-of-the-box win-win options, or some compromise approaching the "equal resistance" model above. The interest-based approach is purpose-built for situations where the relationship after the negotiation must be as strong as before.

I prefer the third option but recommend the interest-based approach augmented by value insights that have developed and built throughout the discovery and selling process…with multiple buying personas. The mutual exchange of value inherent in value-based pricing is a great way to reinforce the outcomes your offer will deliver for a customer. Negotiations tend to become pretty straightforward once the exchange of value is laid out.

A Better Alternative: A Radically Value Focused Company Culture

Disciplined value focus takes company-wide value acumen. It's worth it, but most worth it when you have tools to get you there efficiently and smoothly. Intuitive tools like value networks, business profiles, and value calculators fit the bill.

A value culture is one where customer-centered value assessments permeate all functions of the company. Product development, production, marketing, and even finance understands all value drivers for its products and relies on sales professionals to accurately validate and monetize each value driver with customers. In value-disciplined companies, a wide number of people in varying job roles can list value drivers, tell you why they matter to the customer, and how customers estimate the monetary value of those drivers.

Value focus helps the company more effectively and profitably hone several capabilities:

- **How to market your solution.** High-impact messaging can build on knowing differentiators in detail, then emphasize outcomes. Messaging targeting high-value segments, high-value roles/personas, and describing key outcomes is at the core of impactful content. Using the universal language of value internally facilitates that.

- **How to sell your solution.** When sellers understand customer value, they add critical depth to their selling strategies. They predict which different buying influences, personas, or roles highly value your solution. Then, they leverage that knowledge into more effective selling strategies.

- **Where to sell your solution.** Knowing which customers map to which differentiators and outcomes guide sellers to more profitable, defensible customers. Market segmentation decisions have a powerful impact.

- **How to price your solution purposefully.** Value-centric pricing is not just for custom or semi-custom products. Companies using value discipline can set standard pricing that reflects full value to customers. Sales forces use value-centric price methodologies to resist discounting from original quotes. When a customer estimates that your product increases their profits by $1MM more than any other option, Purchasing's insistence on a $20,000 price concession can be politely and productively placed into proper perspective with nobody losing face (or accepted with full, objective knowledge why it was necessary).

- **More profitable, differentiated product development.** Value-focused conversations between sales, marketing, and product groups achieve clarity and efficiency. Value discipline used along with methodologies like Agile etc. is especially powerful. Product re-engineering and cost-engineering should use value discipline as guardrails. While all companies aspire to efficient and effective new product management, those who have a common language of value between customers, sales, and product groups can do so more seamlessly.

- **Resource allocation decisions are regularly based upon value to the enterprise.** Instead, *value to the customer* forms an ideal filter for various resource requests. I used the example earlier of one company, which forces all prototype requests, no matter how simple, to be forced over a customer value hurdle. For instance, "we won't sign drawings (much less commit any build resources) unless value will command at least a 20% price premium over the best competitor".

- **Well-conducted value discussions *increase customer loyalty* at higher prices.** A component that shortens the preventative maintenance downtime for a large industrial machine can be worth many times the price of its competitor when customers account for the revenue from increased production hours every month. Actively conducting that discussion with the customer is the only way they'll connect that component with their business outcome.

As you can see, while value discipline delivers powerful outcomes when Sales organizations adopt it, the benefits of integrating it into the weave of the overall corporate culture deliver long-term results that few other initiatives can match.

The Challenge: Implementation and Change Management

Putting value at the center of your company focus is the kernel inside of the buzzword "customer focus."

I've shared readily-implemented tools to help your organization focus on customer value. Implementing selling methodology is straightforward but not always easy. *The big challenge isn't in the methodologies or the tools themselves;* it's making the changes to organizational behavior required to incorporate the methodologies into the company's operating rhythm. *The challenge is change management.*

Key Questions in Change Management

A former colleague of mine, Rich Blakeman, was the veteran of scores of change management initiatives. He identifies[54] several key questions to be considered when formulating change management. When the change is sales methodology alone, these questions require well-crafted answers. When the change is sales

---

[54] The Hybrid Sales Channel, Rich Blakeman

methodology plus the customer value focus tools, the answers almost write themselves…but here are his five questions:

"Is there a connection between the change and an overall strategy?"

The tools I've described form the connection between methodology and a culture of customer value. When you add value focus tools, the change *is* the connection. Customer value focus is intuitively easy to grasp, and people tend to be relieved that the tools used are easy to master and use.

"Is there a connection between the individual and his or her impact on the strategy and its goals?"

I've described how value networks and offer value statements are a basis of customer discussions. I've described how a wide variety of roles within the organization contribute to delivering a deeper understanding of customer value. The value assessment draws a bright, direct, measurable line between customer value and a value driver.

"Is there an attempt to show individuals how they can make a difference and how that will impact them personally, professionally, and especially (in sales) financially?"

Value focus creates a closed-loop between each individual's role and the success of the company. Giving workers this view empowers higher performance and focuses everyone in the organization on not just the customer, but customer value: the aspect of the customer the organization exists to affect.

"Is there a structured, ongoing communication process that extends beyond the initial presentations, slide decks, and high-level emails?"

Value focus tools are meant to communicate value intelligence company-wide; the tools themselves are the communication process. There does need to be a robust plan to implement the tools in an operating cadence. We've talked about how value focus is coached, but leaders need to 1) learn how to coach and 2) change their coaching behavior by adding value focus into their operating rhythm. 3) lead by example.

"Are there metrics that tie individual performance to the overall performance of the change?"

There should be metrics around how well we understand customer-perceived value. Look to the Value Assessment for that, and to any relevant value networks to see how thoroughly customer value is understood by your organization (not just your sales team). The beauty is that customer perceived value is something we all understand intuitively. The value focus tools are meant to align with our human processes, not change them. There are certainly some habits to be changed, but they don't feel forced or uncomfortable.

Where is Your Company in its Value Focus Journey?

I'm passionate about value focus. I welcome your questions about how to implement it in your organization, or how to adapt it to your business model and your culture. Your investment of time to read this book speaks more to me than the money you spent to buy it. If I can honor that time investment with further discussions, I welcome them. Feel free to reach me at mark@boundyconsulting.com

To your success!

Key Take-Aways

Corporate Leaders: Any change is hard. Shifting your company to value focus is, on the one hand, a comprehensive change that touches every corner of the enterprise. On the other hand, it's pretty intuitive and easy to lead by example. It's also compelling: it engages everyone in your company into the process of producing value for your customers.

Sales Leaders: This book is all about how to gather the entire company around customer perceived value. The good news: your organization is the spotlight. The bad news: your organization is in the spotlight. I've described and presented tools that will make this culture change initiative easier, but your leadership will be demanded.

Sales Enablement and Sales Operations Leaders: A bulk of the change management burden for a value-focus initiative may fall on you since sellers are at the epicenter of value focus. Value focus is a company-wide discipline, and you will need to learn the language of other job disciplines in your organizations, no matter how much or little of the burden you end up absorbing.

This is a burden, obviously, but it's also an opportunity to become more networked around your organization. Change management is a difficult job. If you haven't conducted a successful initiative before, reach out to anyone you know who has for help and pointers. If you have conducted a successful change management initiative, figure out what you can repeat and try to spot differences so that you can get anticipate challenges. I'm happy to help. Feel free to reach out.

Sellers: I'm asking you to think about selling and about your customers in a new way. I'm also asking you to have in-depth conversations about subjects you may not have ever explored with them before. This system works. It will make you better, more valued by your customers, a more successful salesperson, and should give you greater satisfaction. It also asks you to change a lot of habits. Be open, be coachable, be motivated.

Marketing Professionals: Like sales, I'm asking you to think about marketing, sales and about your customers in a new way. I'm also asking you to explore subjects you may not have explored before: business acumen, outcome-based communication, value verification, and monetization. You have a crucial part in shifting your company to value focused.

Product/Service Professionals: If you think of your products or services as a means for customers to achieve great (new) things in their lives, we are kindred spirits. The products and services in your care provide the revenue streams that keep your companies alive. New products and product enhancements are the succession plan for your company's revenue streams. Focusing on what outcomes they provide in the lives of your customers, and how they value those outcomes...that's why your business is in business. Embrace customer value and help those around you embrace it. The tools in this book will help.

About the Author

Mark Boundy has grown businesses in a variety of industries for 25 years, amassing wide-ranging experience in sales, marketing, new product development, and product management. He helps his clients find, win, and keep more business—more profitably. He's led firms to be value – and price – leaders in a wide variety of product and service industries.

Growing businesses within W.L.Gore & Associates (makers of Gore-Tex®), Lucent Technologies, and GE Capital, Mark developed highly differentiated, premium-priced offerings in some thought-to-be-commodity businesses (like electrical cable and money). He started Boundy Consulting, LLC, to leverage his expertise to clients, mostly in the sales performance area. Ultimately, he formed ValuClarity, packaging his expertise into courses and consulting methodologies available electronically and through affiliates.

Mark holds a degree with high distinction in Business Administration from the University of Michigan's Ross Business School. He lives in Phoenix, Arizona, father of two grown sons. He is an avid mountain biker and culinary hobbyist.

To learn more about Mark's services, contact mark@boundyconsulting.com or visit www.BoundyConsulting.com.